Other books by Karla Telega:

Box of Rocks
A Maggie Gorski Mystery

Published by
Tart Cookies Press / March 2013

Tart Cookies Press
Moncks Corner, SC
telegatales.com

Copyright © 2013 by Karla Telega
All rights reserved.

Published in the United States by Tart Cookies Press

Names, characters, places, and incidents are the product of the author's imagination, or are used fictitiously. Any resemblance to actual events, locales, or persons, living or dead is entirely coincidental.

No part of this book may be reproduced or transmitted in any form or by any means, electronic or mechanical, including photocopying, recording, or by any information storage and retrieval system, without permission in writing from the publisher. For information, address: Tart Cookies Press

ISBN 978-0-9848003-3-9

I Never Drove a Bulldozer

There's a Hole in my Bucket List

Karla Telega

Tart Cookies Press

telegatales.com

*Dedicated with love to
Dave, Bekki, and Michelle.*

*Thank you for never letting me
take myself too seriously.*

Introduction

I never used to read the introduction, preface, or acknowledgements in any book, so if you decide to skip this section, I won't hold it against you. Just don't blame me later if you miss any important housekeeping announcements. (The bathrooms are out the double doors, to your right.) The introduction does not include plot exposition, reference material, or handy laundry tips. Please be assured that no research sources were harmed in the making of this book. I need to include the standard disclaimer: any resemblance of characters or circumstances in this book to actual events or people is purely coincidental. For the nonstandard disclaimer: I will not be held responsible for any chainsaw massacres, petty larceny, fashion faux pas, or generally bad life-choices made as a result of reading this book.

If you're still reading, my purpose in writing this book is twofold:
- To supplement my income (See *Financial Preparations for a Penniless Retirement*)
- I forget the other one (See *Where did I Leave my Memories?*)

This being my first book, I asked my family to read the outline and let me know their honest thoughts. My kids laughed at me, and my husband shrugged. Needless to say, there will be no acknowledgements for their support and understanding. I would like to tip my hat to one of my greatest sources of inspiration for this project: Erma Bombeck. Over the years, her unerring ability to make me laugh kept me sane through some rocky stretches in my life. If you don't believe me, I can get a note from my psychiatrist.

Were you impressed with the way I snuck some of the acknowledgements into the introduction? You can thank me now for sparing you another section you probably won't read.

"Why," you might ask, "would you write a book about aging?" If you watch TV, you will see a lot of advertising geared toward the baby boomers. This generation has proven to be a lucrative demographic, so every TV program is punctuated by at least one commercial hawking remedies for overactive bladders. Please be assured I would never stoop to pandering to such a large percentage of the population, even if they are attractive, and sophisticated enough to read books replete with pathos, angst, and excellent punctuation. By the way, that sweater is very becoming on you.

I'm hoping a large print edition of the book will be published. This will help those people who have forgotten where they put their reading glasses and who have short arms. I also take a keen personal interest in the effect of squinting on crows' feet.

If at any time this book causes you insomnia, excessive thirst, or toe fungus, I have a team of lawyers standing by to dither around in court until you give up on your class action suit. Just sayin'.

Chapter 1
Playing Well with Others

Unless you are the Unibomber, you're going to find yourself in the company of other people. Our relationships can either evolve as we grow older, or become a special three-part series on the Jerry Springer show. Grown children find ways to get back at you for not letting them keep that stray kitten. Many marriages fracture, leaving us to suck in our guts and seek companions who prefer to make love with the lights off. If you move to a retirement community, you might be stuck with the same annoying neighbor until buzzards circle her house. Co-workers ten years your junior, who developed a career while you were canning pickles and boiling cloth diapers, are now your bosses. You can either deal with change, or get used to writing manifestos and cleaning litter boxes.

Chapter 1

I raised my kids wrong on purpose because it was funny

I never dared to pee in the sink when I was a child. I grew up in a gentler time, when my parents could smack the snot out of their kids with impunity. Mom even went so far as to say she liked using a wooden spoon because it "stung really good without leaving a mark." Most muggings are not planned out so well. My parents taught me good principles, which I failed to pass along to my children. We'll just call it an "oversight," since "negligence" carries specific legal ramifications.

My answer to the wooden spoon was the "smacking glove." It was my weapon of choice on long car drives. I would reach back and flail blindly in the kids' general direction, while they scooted back, and plastered themselves against the seat, giggling. It was my version of seatbelt-light: half the annoyance, zero protection. My battle cry of "Don't make me get my smacking glove!" failed to impress the girls as they got older. It was time to pull out the big guns.

I was a believer in natural consequences. When my youngest daughter was in eighth grade and expelled from public school for a year, I had to find a private school. As a consequence, I sent her to a school with ugly uniforms. The next year, when she returned to public school, she received a good citizen award. Is there a correlation between dress code and ethical behavior? You be the judge.

Sometimes, what seemed like capricious malice on my part was just my ignorance of basic childrearing etiquette. As long as my feet are on the curb, does it matter that my baby stroller is sticking out onto the crosswalk? If I allow my toddler to feed grass to a horse, at what point should I yank her hand out of the horse's mouth?

On a trip to the office supply store, I loaded my paper into the car and started for home. I was across the parking lot and about to turn onto the main road when I looked at the empty seat next to me and thought, "That doesn't look right." I realized what was missing as soon as my 16 year-old daughter opened the door, out of breath, and scowled at me. I should have been horrified at forgetting my child, but laughed until snot came out of my nose. To this day, she rushes to put away the shopping cart while I gun the engine.

Oddly, my kids thank me for the principles I taught them. They seem to have a completely different recollection of those halcyon days than I do.

My daughter's memory: We gave back to the community by delivering Thanksgiving dinners to those in need.

Chapter 1

My memory: My daughter stood in the doorway, asking in a loud voice, "Is this where the poor people live?"

My girls insist that back in the day, I was strict.

My memory: My daughter stood at the bottom of the stairs and shouted up to me, "I'm going out to party and experiment with recreational drugs with my friends."

"Just be home by midnight." I answered. "Tomorrow's a school day."

"No promises. We might hang out on the street corner downtown after the party."

"You know the rule." I reminded her. "If you can't make curfew, call at midnight and let me know where you are."

She was fourteen at the time. "And the award for worst parent in a starring role goes to … "

The little nipper insists she could never get away with the same stuff at our house that she did at her friends' houses, which would have been more comforting if she had not spent most of her time at her friends' houses. She feels like an idiot now because she actually *did* check in at midnight and told me truthfully where she was. Okay, once it was the police who called, but that still counts as making curfew.

Despite their unfortunate upbringing, my kids have turned out to be delightful adults. They are caring, thoughtful, and they don't pee in the sink (to my knowledge).

May - December relationships

Several years ago, as I was getting my nipple pierced (See *Mid-Life Madness*), the nineteen year-old tattoo parlor tech, Justin, told me younger men are attracted to older women. He added that he and several of his friends had discussed the subject at length and came to the same conclusion. I can just imagine the conversation.

"Hey Dude," Justin said. "I just had this old woman come in. She totally wanted me."

"I've heard those old chicks know how to do stuff that would set your shorts on fire," his friend, Sean answered.

"You're probably not their type, Sean. You're not exactly a chick magnet."

"Like that matters. These ladies go for anything with a pulse and an Adam's apple. They can't wait to get their hands on real studs."

First of all, what could possibly prompt such a vulgar topic of conversation among the maturity impaired?

Hormones and alcohol.

Secondly, was Justin under the influence of said hormones and alcohol while poking one of my most tender lady parts with an ice pick?

Chapter 1

The odds are pretty good.

I've read that a man's sex drive peaks around eighteen, then steadily declines over the rest of his life. A woman's sex drive doesn't peak; it just increases all her life. Who makes up these statistics? My sex drive might be snowballing, but I just can't squeeze into the French maid outfit anymore. Turns out it only takes chafing lace to put the brakes on an intimate evening.

Sex with a younger man would be like the recent changes to my taste in food. The older I get, the more I love hot spicy food. While my taste buds are asking for zing, my stomach is asking for mercy.

Can a May-December relationship work out? The three or four women I have polled on the subject agree that older women and young men don't mix. There are a few exceptions to the rule. I'm sure these women have many fine qualities and great personalities; but whether by nature or by suture, being gorgeous at 50 doesn't hurt.

My tattoo tech's parting shot was that he would be happy to "make my dreams come true" if I was interested.

"Are you available on Saturday?" I asked.

"Yes," he jumped in. "What time should I come?"

"If you come over early enough, you'll have time to mow the lawn after you wash my car."

Crash and burn in Hell

After that last section, you might think I'm some kind of pervert. In reality, I was the Church Lady ... literally. Don't worry, I'm not going to come over there and smack you in the head with my Bible.

My relationship with God has become increasingly private as I've aged. Until recently, I never missed a Sunday going to church. I worked six years as a parish administrator in a large and busy Episcopal church. I attended community Bible Studies and retreats, sang in the choir, and made cookies for the coffee hour. Any time we moved, our first order of business was to seek out a local family church. It provided us with a seriously bad-ass support network. Episcopalians stop just short of wearing gang colors.

I'm not going to lie. I lived in sin with both of my husbands before marrying them. Even though I believe God forgives such indiscretions, I've always felt a twinge of guilt. I even took my concerns to confession, and Episcopalians don't go to confession lightly. Normally it is reserved for serial murderers who molest goats.

Me: "Bless me, Father, for I have sinned."

Father John: "Cut the Catholic crap and get on with it."

Me: "I have had sex outside of the marital covenant."

Father John: "Did you molest any goats?"

Chapter 1

Me: "No! Who even thinks like that?"

Father John: "Believe me, I get it all the time. God has a special place in hell for farmyard fornicators, but you don't even make the short list. Go forth and be discreet."

Me: "That's it?"

Father John: "Kick some puppies before you come back."

You can't pick your neighbors

In my first marriage of twenty-one years, I was a Navy wife. Every three years I cleaned my closets, held a yard sale, and moved to the city with the highest cost of living in the country. That dubious distinction seemed to follow us up one coast or the other, wherever we lived. Each relocation became more odious than the last, and I dreamed of living in one place long enough to mount my Chevy majestically on blocks in the front yard. After marrying my second husband, we moved to our current home, with the intention of growing old and dying there—preferably in that order. Turns out long term home ownership is as much of a commitment as any other long-term relationship.

I've always tried to be a good and responsible neighbor, but there are some who would snort derisively at that claim. For these neighbors, all you have to do is mow outside the lines, let your Doberman terrorize their

Chihuahua, or run your car over their garbage can, and they become completely unglued. A few profanities, a couple death threats, and before you know it, the tension becomes thick enough to cut with a knife.

I tried the usual placating gestures: talking things out, trying to keep my dogs from barking, having the old Chevy towed out of the yard. There is just no pleasing some people. "Jim" is about the same age as us and was planning on living next door until he died. He just didn't count on his neighbors being inconsiderate boobs with a backyard that smells like a dog urinal on a sunny day.

At some point, you just have to laugh. I've had trouble taking Jim seriously, ever since we were standing and talking in our yards one day, and he said, "You'd better watch your back. I know where you live."

A friend in need is annoying

Multitasking is not my forte. You don't want to be in the car with me if I'm tuning my radio while driving. If I try to chew gum as well, we're talking fourteen-car pile-up. Likewise, I can only manage one close friend at a time.

For the last couple of years I've hit a dry spell in which it's taken up to four days to notice I forgot to turn my cell phone back on after a visit to the doctor's office. This leaves my husband, kids, and gerbil in the unenviable position of having to fill the gaping hole in

Chapter 1

my social life. I prefer to think of it as family bonding rather than social leprosy. You can get away with a lot of bull with your family, but friends don't let friends:

- Drive drunk
- Leave the house with your skirt tucked into your panties
- Fall asleep during the sermon at church
- Dig at your privates in public.

My sour grapes slogan was "Friends are hard. They want your time and your emotional support. They drag you out places you wouldn't normally go."

What a load of crap! The truth is, I just couldn't find a person to take hostage.

TV commercials tell us that as seniors, we should still be hanging out with our lifelong friends. Since I had none, the best I could hope for would be Bingo buddies at the community center. They can't really be considered close friends because they'll cheat as soon as you turn your back. Be sure to watch Andrea Lister like a hawk!

While I was helping my daughter clean up her guesthouse, I zeroed in on her new tenant to be my next best friend forever. I felt like we clicked immediately, but I wasn't sure if she felt the same. I tried to play it cool so she wouldn't think I was some kind of creepy stalker.

"So, would you like to go with me to the hardware store to pick out paint colors?" I asked hopefully.

"Listen, I'm really flattered, but I don't swing that way." Jill explained kindly.

Great, I just suggested we move in together twenty minutes into our friendship. Way to not be creepy.

I tried to salvage the situation. "Oh, you've got it all wrong. I'm just tired of being stuck at home alone …" I just made a sharp right turn at pathetic. " … so I thought we could get some take-out and eat at your new place."

Unfortunately, I'm not built for speed and that girl could move. My only hope was that she'd get a cramp before she made it to the car.

Eventually we cleared up the little misunderstanding, and it wasn't long before we were joyriding through rich neighborhoods and I showed her my favorite hot dog stands. She knows I'm somewhat lacking in class and that I often have conversational constipation, but she likes me anyway. I'd give a kidney for her, as long as it didn't involve hospitals and needles and stuff.

The deep end of the dating pool
I think it's pretty safe to say that over half the marriages in this country end in divorce. I didn't look up the actual percentage, because that would be kind of like research. Marriages of 20 years or more are not immune to this made-up statistic.

Chapter 1

I was one of those women who found themselves back in the deep end of the dating pool after 21 years of marriage. I can't say I had honed my dating skills, because my research for a lifelong mate bears an uncanny resemblance to my research for this book. I managed to find a good guy out of the gate for my first time around the matrimonial maypole, in spite of my lack of effort. Dating before age 20 was a convoluted process, rife with intrigue, jealousy, mystery, and bad hair days:

Playing "does he like me?" with my girlfriends;

Practicing kissing techniques in the mirror;

Hinting of my interest to a potential sweetie.

I made the bold move of waiting outside my quarry's classroom to indicate my undying love. I was concerned he might not like me, but he later told me teenage boys think about sex about once every five seconds. Advantage—Karla! It makes you wonder how boys can tie their shoes or string words together into sentences when they expend so much energy on forbidden fantasies. But I digress.

The dating ritual normally runs for at least two weeks before a couple agrees to go steady. The female participant terminates the early courtship period by writing her pretend married name in different scripts all over her Pee Chee[1].

---

[1] A brown pocket folder, identical in design to every other

I waited long enough before the second time around the dating game, so I had no time for dilly-dallying. The process began when my ex-husband got custody of all our family friends. I eventually got tired of hanging out with my daughters and their friends, so started looking for adult companionship. I did this by:

Allowing a friend to set me up on a blind date;

Making sure my new potential sweetie passed the "cute test;"

Consummating the new relationship on our second date.

Afterwards, my son teased me by sitting on the couch, throwing his feet up in the air and saying, "I'm not that kind of girl!" I didn't know he was so limber.

The early courtship ritual ended with me writing my pretend married name in different fonts on my laptop.

Water cooler comrades

After years of being a stay-at-home mom, I entered the workplace to find a deeper meaning in life at $6 an hour. Like anyone without a police record, I did time as a bank teller. My finest moment in the banking industry was when I was promoted to assistant head teller and received a ten-cent an hour raise. My least fine moment

---

Pee Chee ever made.

Chapter 1

was getting fired for giving away too much of the bank's money. Turns out the front office can't take a little joke.

In a subsequent non-banking job, I was still a little fish in a big pond, surrounded by bosses several years younger than me, but this pond had donut Fridays! Lunchtime was my chance to entertain coworkers with my life story, ignorance of current events, and apathy for anything not related directly to me.

"Kent just got accepted on his college football team," my boss, Mary, said proudly.

"Who's Kent?" I asked.

"My son. I've been talking about him for three years."

"That's a coincidence; I've been working here for three years. How old is he?"

"This is his freshman year in college."

"I loved my freshman year, except my first day when I wandered into the wrong class and they laughed at me. I thought about majoring in accounting, but I didn't do great in Math 101."

Mary looked shocked, "You do trust accounting here!"

"My Uncle Jack was an accountant." I blazed on without missing a beat. "He graduated top of his class before embezzling his company's retirement fund."

"Didn't you mention he went to the same college as Kent?" Mary asked.

"Who's Kent?"

One of the most important dynamics in an office is to designate a "copier un-jammer." This was my calling, destiny, and insurance I would be in the cool crowd. Did I mention I was in the projection club at high school?

In my late forties, I finally took some courses and worked my way up the ladder from tadpole status, until I achieved the ultimate goal of having an office with a real door. Sure, it was a converted storage room, but it was *my* converted storage room. I never forgot the little people who helped me advance in my career, unless I saw them somewhere outside the office setting.

"That woman in produce looks vaguely familiar. Oh, I remember. She's the one who chatted with me in the deli line. It was almost like she knew me."

Five Basic rules for a happy marriage in your golden years:
1. *That toilet seat thing*

An unclosed toilet seat is grounds for divorce in seventeen states, regardless of age. Being a serial toilet seat leaver-upper (that is the technical term) is justification for manslaughter in two states. Set him straight, ladies, if he thinks he can feign dementia to get away with it. Besides the obvious risk factor of falling into the toilet, there's the housekeeping element. As I've

Chapter 1

grown older, I have moved on from keeping my house as neat as a pin to a somewhat more relaxed standard. If I don't have to look at all of the near misses on the bottom of the toilet seat, they don't technically exist.

2. *Slip some Ex-Lax into his brownies*

The "accidental" ingestion of laxatives is a win-win situation. Either he is less cranky because he's regular, or he's spending all his time in the bathroom, avoiding the need for talking to each other. Just so long as he doesn't leave the toilet seat up when he's done.

3. *Tell him, "It happens to every man at one time or another"*

Every woman knows that in a good marriage, we must nurture our man's fragile ego. This is never truer than in this day and age. In modern advertising, men candidly admit to having erectile dysfunction (ED). In real life, men aren't comfortable being so forthcoming. They don't slap each other on the backs and proclaim they've found a great new product their flaccid friends should try. I have never heard erectile dysfunction and NASCAR[2] uttered in the same conversation.

4. *Don't let on that you can read his mind*

I look at my parents as setting an example of a happy marriage, which meant Mom knew everything my Dad

---

[2] Stock car racing. Audience requirement: marriage to your sister.

was thinking. One day, as we were riding in the car, Dad reached over to hold Mom's hand. Mom lovingly placed a roll of Life Savers in his outstretched palm. You can't be on your game every second.

When you invariably slip and finish his sentence, pass it off as a fluke. It will drive him crazy wondering if you know every time he's looking at porn on the internet.

5. **Don't starch his underwear. It's just as true now as it was in Mom's day**

Remember the days before Permanent Press, when liquid starch was used for more things than mixing finger paints? Then, in our lifetime, God created spray starch, and He saw that it was good. No matter how tempting it may be, I recommend you resist the urge to use starch in any form. I've even heard that starching a man's underwear can lead to ED.

Your priorities change as your marriage ripens. My family was exploring a cave in Spain to see the prehistoric cave art deep inside. There were no lighted or paved paths in this cave. We had two tour guides, Socorro and Perdido, with three kerosene lanterns to share between all six of us. I was the family interpreter, so when Perdido pointed out a smudge on the far wall of a cavern and told us it was a bat, I passed it along to the others. It wasn't the highlight of the excursion, but my youngest hadn't seen the smudge, so she started crying.

Chapter 1

Our accommodating guide led us to a 100-meter sink hole, to show us the bats flying in swirling circles deep inside. The opening crevice at the edge of the sinkhole was blocked by one lonely rail. As we approached over the smooth wet rocks, their father forged ahead warning the children, "Be careful, these rocks are slippe …". He grabbed the pole as his feet slid out from under him and swung out over the sinkhole in a move that would rival any gymnast's in grace and agility. I swear, my first thought at that moment was, "Is the life insurance paid up?"

As we get older, passion takes a back seat to practicality.

Is there a point to this?
Relationships can be a pain in the rear. Other people come with baggage and want us to help fix their problems. They have their own agendas, and heaven help you if they get their hands on the remote. They complain, and whine, and get you tacky knick-knacks for your birthdays and Christmas. The remarkable thing about aging is that as your tolerance for human idiocy declines, your friends and family get better, smarter, more charming and more fun to be with. God has a strange sense of humor.

Chapter 2
Change the Locks on your Empty Nest

There comes a time when the chicks are grown and need to leave the nest. Have a little dignity and don't try to lock them in or stalk them in their new homes. Sure, it means you are going to have to relearn the art of adult conversation, and find some way to fill the lonely hours that does not involve scrapbooking their baby teeth. If I had known that getting a dog to replace their affection would involve broken bones on my part, I would have opted for the scrapbooking.

Cutting the Cord
My husband and I feared our kids would be living with us until we were diaper age. To my surprise, as soon as my youngest finished high school, both girls bolted off to get an apartment together. I would now have to travel five minutes away if I wanted to borrow said youngest's black shirt with silver beads. That was worth a little crying.

Chapter 2

When their rent for a crummy apartment got higher than a mortgage payment on a crummy house, they bought a place of their own in a sketchy part of nearby Baltimore. Their new home was half an hour and more tears away. This would definitely make it harder to drop in for surprise inspections. Would I forever be ignorant of their drunken debauchery and high-priced male strippers? Would they forget to invite me?

Soon, the oldest got married and decided to move out of state; I started to hyperventilate. Later, my youngest called to tell me she was interested in moving to the same area, and I was rummaging around the garage for the "For Sale" sign before I hung up the phone. My husband and I quit our jobs, sold our house, found a vacant lot about half an hour away from the girls' houses, and started building. Until then, my biggest impulse buy had been a swoop for the last York Peppermint Patty in the supermarket checkout line.

With all the expensive bells and whistles we put into it, our new house is valued at less than what we paid. We could sell the house tomorrow, for the price of some fine swampland in South Carolina, so I hope the girls don't move anytime soon. I can write off the first time I followed them as "I came to visit and really liked the area!" Since it would involve the sale of multiple internal organs to make up for a loss on the sale of our house, the next time I move across country to be in my mandatory half an hour zone is going to look pathetic and creepy, and require regular dialysis.

Maybe someday the kids will be able to cut the cord on Mom. If all else fails, they can accidentally forget me in a mall parking lot.

How to talk "Grown-up"
When children move away from home, they take with them your money, your personal possessions, and your conversational skills. I've never been able to switch mental gears easily, so arguments about curfews are never going to morph into discussions on global warming. I haven't read a newspaper since I first started reading Sandra Boynton books to my children. I can still recite *Moo, Baa, La-La-La* by heart, but I can't tell you the name of our Secretary of Defense.

So where do you start? There's always the option of email. With the internet, one may express oneself with eloquent detail and literacy. ☺ When my husband and I decide to resort to email, we have to take turns using the office chair, since our computers are right next to each other.

My husband can solve the New York Times crossword puzzle, but he has never been big on verbal communication. Over the years, I've learned to

Chapter 2

differentiate between a "yes" grunt and a "no" grunt. If you insist on talking to one another, my advice is to start small:

"Which brand of chicken soup is the best?" My husband asked. Beads of sweat formed on his upper lip at the exertion of uttering a complete sentence.

"How should I know?" It came to me right then that he was trying to start a conversation. Since this might lead to a deeper connection on a spiritual level, I didn't want to blow the opportunity. "I guess it depends on what kind of chicken soup you mean. Are we talking chicken noodle, chicken and rice, chicken gumbo, or cream of chicken?"

"There's a coupon in the paper, but there's no point in using it if we don't like the brand."

Aha! Now we were getting somewhere. Quick, think of something he can relate to. "Brand loyalty is like a football game. If the offense is lining up in the shotgun, the defense shouldn't go five in the secondary."

"I don't see the connection between the two; and since when do you know anything about defense?"

(Cricket, cricket, cricket ...)

"Women have a more complicated bathroom routine than men, so there should be more Ladies rooms in stadiums!" (Men, if you want to avoid this subject, don't ever start with "What kept you?")

My husband stood and walked out of the room without another word. What could I do? When the big moment came—I choked.

Opening with any more substantial topic than soup would be like working without a net your first time on the trapeze. If you find working the trapeze less intimidating than trying to make clever conversation, you and your spouse could later talk about the rising cost of health care ... while you're in the emergency room.

Get a Dog. Need I say more?
As I was waiting for a chiropractor appointment, I read a book on simplifying your life. It had a section devoted to getting a dog. The premise was that the benefits of exercise and companionship would outweigh the added responsibilities of dog ownership. I wasn't sure this was a compelling argument at the time. It made about as much sense as hanging your clothes out to dry in Seattle, but I felt a cult-like attraction to many of the other tenets of downsizing covered in the book, so I tucked it away into the section of my brain devoted to advertising jingles. (My brain works on the Dewey Decimal System).

1. ***Picking the Breed***

A year and a half into our simple lifestyle, I had an attempted break-in, which occurred minutes after my husband left for work. Were they watching the house?

Chapter 2

Since my geriatric Sheltie had not bothered to wake up through the commotion, I decided at that moment, "We're going to need a bigger dog." I perused the yellow pages for rental Rottweilers without success, so I posted a sign warning that the house was protected by ninjas, and took my daughter's Rottie on loan until I could get a dog of my own.

Not being the hands-on type, I prepared for this life-changing event by dumping the job of researching different breeds onto my daughter. She also helped me find a breeder, and to sacrifice hundreds of dollars to the gods of retail merchandising on puppy paraphernalia. I chose a Doberman Pinscher because they were easy to train, loyal, and loving family members, and the subject of many a bad guy's nightmare. What my daughter's research didn't find is that Dobies are among the ten most flatulent breeds of dog: an unfortunate oversight.

My cute little puppy, Colt, is now off the growth charts for Dobermans, weighing in at 120 pounds. He's not exactly fearless. When confronted by a German Shepherd, a stranger, or a dust bunny, he hides as much as his bulk he can squeeze behind me. He eats his way through 50-pound bags of designer dog food faster than I can hoist them into the car trunk, and snacks on his own poop between meals. Colt stretches across the whole couch when he's sleeping. As it turns out, "simplifying your life," means that smaller is better. Oops!

2. *Favorite Child*

Some women act as if they had personally squirted out their newborn puppy progeny. Whenever I saw "Mommy" giving "Sweetums" a cookie on dog training shows or in the park, I just wanted to slap them and say, "What's the matter with you?" That was before I got my own little bundle of fleas.

My kids have no illusions about their place in the pecking order; their new little brother is obviously Mommy's favorite child. Yes, I have become one of those lunatics who want to nurture their dog's inner puppy. Colt has his "blankies" and "babies," which he eats as eagerly as if they were made of poop. Once, this led to a close brush with surgery for an intestinal blockage, so now I monitor his stuffed animal consumption much more carefully. I think we've already pretty well established that I'm bad at the mom-stuff.

The aforementioned Rottweiler, which I borrowed from my daughter, was my first grand-dog. I spoiled him on the weekends before sending him home to Mom and Dad. Skeeter is becoming a low energy dog as he gets older, but he'll still perk up when he hears, "grandma," or "pie." Say them both together in a sentence, and he wets himself.

Chapter 2

Once I turned my back on Skeeter with a pan of apple cobbler on the counter. The little mutt was brazen enough to eat the cobbler out of the pan while I stood in the same room with him. When I scolded him and went to shoo him off the counter, he hunkered his face in and slurped it up faster. Obviously, I'm not ready for real grandchildren, when I can't even control a 100-pound cobbler-crazed Rottweiler on a sugar high.

3. ***Exercise and Companionship***

I knew that owning a big dog meant I would have to train him very well. Osteoporosis and 120 pounds of excited muscle on a leash don't mix. I started to walk Colt twice a day from the beginning, in order to establish myself as the pack leader. We got to the point where he behaved pretty well on the walks ... and I got cocky.

One day, when my youngest daughter was visiting me, her two dogs decided to act up. Obviously, all they needed was exercise with a strong pack leader. The next day, while my daughter was at work, I went to her house and saddled up her dogs. I thought that Colt would be a calming influence to the others on the walk. If Cesar Milan could handle walking ten dogs or more at a time, I should be able to manage three. The flaw in that theory is that I was walking an English Mastiff, a Chow Mix, and a Doberman. The mastiff weighed more than me. Taking Cesar's advice, I visualized the outcome I wanted and stepped outside. Things started to go badly before I made it off the front porch.

By the time I wrestled the dogs to the street, I knew this could not end well. We had hardly been out five seconds, and the next-door neighbor's dogs ran to the fence and started barking. I was airborne before I knew it, watching the pavement come up at me with alarming speed. The emergency room doctor was impressed I managed to break my shoulder in three places merely from walking dogs.

It turns out dog ownership is a very good way to simplify your life. I spent the next six weeks sitting on the couch, trying to find a comfortable position, and then not moving. You can't get much simpler than that.

Get a Hobby
If you are still having trouble conversing with your spouse, nothing fills the silence better than a table saw and a death wish. Since woodworking is not my forte, I decided the birds could find their own damn houses. In an effort to avoid playing solitaire, pondering my existence, and picking my belly button lint after the kids moved out, I started dreaming up possible activities that didn't include parlor games, toenail clippings, or accidental dismemberment.

Chapter 2

I believe all seniors with their original hips should take up ballroom dancing. You and your significant other will learn teamwork, timing, and if you're lucky, the dip. If you're not lucky, you might have to replace your original hips.

Television commercials would have you believe that most active seniors spend their time surfing and skydiving. Let's be realistic. The most athletic activity I've witnessed is golf and collectables. You can always break the mold by taking up skeet shooting. If it's an Olympic sport, we should be safe calling it exercise. This also opens the door for collectable multi-tasking. When the Franklin Mint comes out with their first double-barreled sawed-off shotgun with the likeness of Elvis etched in 100%, 24-carat gold on the rifle stock, you can be the first to own this valuable collector's item. The problem is, if walking dogs doesn't break my other shoulder, the kickback on the shotgun will.

Since my second (and current) husband can eat pretty much anything, I've started cooking dinners again. Move over pot pies and fish sticks. I use meat in styrofoam trays with plastic wrap, and occasionally shop in the produce department. Sometimes an empty nest can bring out a perverse and vindictive side of me. I still don't like to cook, but if it annoys the kids because they didn't get real food while they were living at home, it is time well spent.

If you need a more traditional hobby, may I suggest either rabbit breeding or philately? They're practically interchangeable, although I can't think of a real-life example. If stamp collecting turns out not to be your thing, you can wallpaper the rabbit hutch with stamps. I hear that licking the glue gets the little fuzz balls quite randy. If rabbit husbandry turns out not to be your thing, you may have to fall back on your firearms collection and cooking. May I suggest Hasenpfeffer?

Personally, I'm no weekend warrior. Ever since my mastiff marathon landed me in the emergency room, I've become much more cautious. You can keep your kite boarding and model rocketry; my favorite hobbies are reading, writing, and reality shows. I especially like any ghost hunting shows. If I could stay awake past midnight and had better bladder control, I would enjoy going on a paranormal investigation.

Sometimes a hobby can take a heartwarming and life-affirming turn. Generally, I am too self-absorbed to play well with others, so it came as a great surprise when I got a totally altruistic obsession upon seeing my dog interact with a senior outside Uber-Mart. I decided to train Colt to be a therapy dog.

Chapter 2

After watching Cesar Milan and Victoria Stilwell,[3] I started training Colt in earnest. He passed his first test and received his "AKC Canine Good Citizen Award." Next, we would do the testing to become a registered therapy dog. I visualized the outcome: Colt in bed spooning with an 85 year-old. I'm confident there is nothing like snuggling a Doberman to lower blood pressure and promote relaxation. It turns out Colt does not share my philosophy. He feels there is nothing more terrifying than old people, wheelchairs, and assisted living centers. Since I can hardly avoid getting old myself, there may come a day when I have to pin bacon to my clothes in order to get my dog to come near me.

See the world (or at least Kentucky)
Another good way to fill those empty hours is by traveling. When it all got too much for her, my Mom gave me her motor home. I'm not going to turn down a free recreational vehicle, but this RV can only be described as "vintage." We're lucky to have lap belts. Advantages to camping in an RV:
- Not sleeping on the ground
- Lower rates for a camping site than for a motel room

---

[3] Please, somebody take the remote before I become a danger to myself or others.

- Freedom to smoke, drink, watch porn, and enjoy the wilderness from the temperature-controlled comfort of your mini living room.

Disadvantages:

- Unhooking and taking your whole house to a restaurant if you want to go out to dinner
- Walking to the public restroom for number two, so you don't clog up your tank
- Heart attacks at the gas pumps
- More places for the dog to get carsick.

I have the unfortunate habit of being too proud to admit that taking my turn at driving is hard. I won't even tell my husband when the headlights have gotten so dim I can't see the road. I just lean closer to the windshield like a myopic bat, hoping those ten inches of extra distance will keep me out of the ditch. Driving the motor home is similar to my dog-walking, in that I visualize the positive outcome before I climb behind the wheel of a couple tons of steel. What's the worst that could happen? In all my years of driving, I've only ripped the tailpipe off once, and those traffic cones had it coming.

Our most recent trip was working our way through the Appalachians. Somewhere between the Colonel Sanders museum in Corbin, Kentucky and the Bob Evans Farm in Ohio (my husband planned the itinerary), I found the shortcut from hell.

Chapter 2

After a 45-minute delay for re-grading, I proceeded down the most narrow lanes in which you could not possibly pass an oncoming truck without it becoming a hood ornament; and ended with a death-defying leap over railroad tracks, rivaling any car chase scene from *The Streets of San Francisco*. Our motor home became airborne and bottomed out repeatedly, while dragging the truck we were towing behind us. My husband worried about our undercarriage, while I worried about our Yellowstone coffee mugs. We can replace the tailpipe (again) but we might never make it back to Yellowstone Park.

In that moment, I would have preferred being one of the people on the town's sidewalk, doubled over with hysterical laughter, to being behind the wheel soiling myself with terror. At least the Yellowstone mugs survived.

Buy a new ride
When my oldest daughter first got her driver's license, we bought a compact car with a lot of miles on it, but it was very clean and in good condition. By the time it had gone through both of my kids and was ready to be retired, it looked like an army of Mongols had camped in it for a month. Even the best of cars is no match for a teenager with a learner's permit and a need for freedom.

By the time my kids moved out, we were all driving clunkers.

If you're not bankrupt by the time you've paid for senior proms, college text books, and tuition, then it's time to get a new car. Your first empty nester car gives you the possibility to go small and sporty, or settle for a big, bad 4-wheel drive. You can look for a car that's economical, sexy looking, eco-friendly, or the same color as your favorite nail polish.

Empty Nester Ride Guide
A. When grocery shopping do you:
   1. Go every day for a few items, taking your own cloth bags?
   2. Buy one week's worth of groceries at a time?
   3. Buy the large economy-size paper towels, toilet paper, peanut butter, etc.?
   4. Have a one-year supply of food stockpiled at all times?
B. Your favorite outing is:
   1. A night at the opera
   2. Good seats to see a football game
   3. Watching NASCAR on your buddy's big screen TV
   4. A family reunion
C. Do you vote:

Chapter 2

1. Party line Republican?
2. Bi-partisan?
3. Party line Democrat?
4. Independent?

D. Your home is located:
1. Downtown
2. Suburbs
3. Rural
4. Utah

E. When choosing a dress do you:
1. Check the latest fashions and have one tailor-made?
2. Go to a nice boutique?
3. Buy off the rack at a department store?
4. Lay in a supply of plastic trash bags and duct tape from the dollar store?

Using the number next to each answer you chose, add together total points for the five questions.

If your score was:

1 – 4   You are not the sharpest tool in the shed.

5 – 9   Go straight to the nearest Mercedes dealership.

10 – 14 You'll want to buy one of the many compact eco-friendly "smart" cars on the market.

15 – 19	Look for a full size truck with a Hemi or trail-rated Jeep. 4-Wheel Drive is a must.
20	You are Mormon and probably have 18 children. You will never be an empty nester and should settle for a refurbished school bus.

A room with a view

I was not an only child, and I'm not the parent of an only child (POOC). I was in high school when I got a room of my own, and it was the day after I moved out that Mom and Dad changed the locks and converted my room into a place where they could get naked and steamy: a sauna. If you are a POOC, try to resist the temptation to maintain your child's room exactly as it was. Where you see sentimental, the rest of us see Norman Bates.

If you need inspiration check out the game, "Clue."[4] You can convert your child's room into a library, billiard room, or conservatory. Just be sure not to store ropes, candlesticks, or lead pipes in the room.

"Hey, Babe," my husband said. "Why don't we put those boxes of cannibalized computer parts from IBM 386's into Jen's room?"

---

[4] "Cluedo" to all the free world except America. What do you expect from a society too lazy to say, "laughing out loud." LOL

Chapter 2

"I thought we threw those away 20 years ago," I countered.

"We wouldn't want to miss this opportunity for extra storage space."

I couldn't believe he was going to push the issue! Storage? "Let's compromise. We'll take up a hobby we both enjoy and convert Jen's room into a rec room. We could set up some rabbit hutches in there."

"That would be the perfect place to display my small arms collection."

"Then it's settled. We'll keep firearms and small game animals in the room. What could go wrong?"

When all else fails, think outside the box. Knock out a wall and convert your child's room into a garage. Then you have a great place to start your middle-aged chick band. While other POOCs are dusting porcelain dolls, you and your girlfriends will be laying down Bangles tunes. If the homeowners' association comes with torches and pitchforks, pass out some suspicious brownies. They will show their appreciation of your hospitality by waving their torches back and forth as you sing *Eternal Flame*.

Take up Poker so you can play the guilt card

When I remarried I learned that my husband had an annual New Year's Eve poker party. I hope I'm not arrested when I say it was the first time I'd ever played for money. I was making out pretty good—up $1.26!

My son enjoys the occasional game of Five Card Stud, so he joined us. Once we got some young blood in the game, my girls got interested. Soon they were drawn to the table like flies to poop. This was my chance to ambush them!

I have tried with limited success throughout my children's formative years to shame them into doing my bidding. Now that they can see through my machinations, I'm not sure why I continue to try. It annoys me when my mother tries to play the guilt card on me, but I feel like I have to pay it forward to my kids.

Me: "You never call."

Daughter: "You came over to visit yesterday."

Me: "I've been having these strange pains. It's probably nothing."

Daughter: "Time to reign in the hypochondria."

Me: "If it's not too much trouble ..." with the right note of sarcasm.

Daughter: "The guilt card didn't work when I was ten. What makes you think it's going to work now?"

Me: "Don't make me get my smacking glove!"

Grandchildren – Don't go there

I have no idea why parents push their children into giving them grandchildren. First of all, I've got the gray

Chapter 2

hair to prove I'm getting on in years. If I pay out the nose for a brilliant hairdresser to keep my roots under control, only to have some snot-nosed kid call me "grandma" in public – then I'm out of the closet. It's too late by then to leave him at the bus station.

I'm pretty sure I would fail the physical exam for grandparenthood. I can't pick up loads over twenty pounds, I would never make it from the front porch to the street in under six seconds, I can only assume two of the seven basic ballet moves, and I cannot hold my breath for longer than forty seconds (not nearly enough time to change a dirty diaper). Discipline is not my strong suit, and I would buy a pony for just five minutes of peace and quiet.

I spent twenty-one years turning my children into responsible adults. Why would I want to start over from scratch? I have all the usual excuses for not wanting to deal with small children:

- They poop their pants
- They scream incessantly over nothing
- They can sometimes be "Children of the Corn" creepy
- They can say the darnedest things. (Art Linkletter's euphemism for "Damned embarrassing").

OK, I suppose babies are cute, and they say that kids keep you young. (When you use the word, "they" in this context, you don't have to prove your point.) It would also be nice to have someone to carry on the family name or to inherit all your recessive genes.

I guess kids do have some redeeming qualities:
- They look angelic when they're sleeping
- They can keep you on your toes and feeling young
- They give hugs freely and often
- They can say the cutest things.

So what's wrong with my kids that they don't want to squirt out babies? Don't they know the years of hardships they'll endure so I can have hours of fun? I'd play the guilt card on this one, but I think they're on to me.

Chapter 3
It's All in Your Head

One of the most common medical conditions for seniors is hypochondria. I currently have to take pills as between meal snacks, so I don't ruin my appetite. Where Mom used to diagnose my childhood ills, we now have WebMD and television commercials. Information age medicine may be more expensive than Mom, and cause an erection lasting more than four hours, but at least it doesn't involve laxatives for a stubbed toe. As seniors, we have the opportunity to practice medicine on our grandchildren. We can try to pass off their head lice as dandruff and terrify them with stories of toilet seat cooties. It's not the same as laxatives, but you've got to pay it forward somehow.

Hypochondria – hī-pə-kŏn-drē-ə. 1. *Psychiatry.* an excessive preoccupation with one's health, usually focusing on some particular symptom, such as cardiac or gastric symptoms. 2. excessive worry or talk about one's health.

My sciatica is acting up
Have you noticed how diseases of the elderly have ridiculous names and are hard to spell? I didn't know and didn't care what Grandma Saari's sciatica was. Now that I've experienced it myself, a brief mention in a letter is like calling a shark attack "just a scratch."

I'm pretty sure there is no special reward in heaven for stoicism, so my friends and family are going to know every ache and pain I'm experiencing, which is at least as interesting as enduring grandpa's endless photos of sunsets. I think it's safe to say I can take full credit for the new drive-through window at the doctor's office.

One of the advantages of keeping your general malaise in the limelight is that you can more easily beg off from steam cleaning the rug, washing the windows, and cleaning the toilet. Where you might call it "lazy," I call it "motivationally challenged."

"I can't really help with the yard work today. My brain tumor has been acting up." I sighed dramatically.

My husband wasn't buying it. "Weeding the garden won't aggravate a tumor."

"Are you kidding me? Any exertion could cause an aneurysm to explode in my skull."

Chapter 3

He glanced up. "Have you been having headaches?"

"No."

"How's your blood pressure been?"

"Borderline, but the doctor said recent research suggests that borderline is the new high."

He shook his head. "If you finish the weeding, I'll have some flowers to bring to your funeral."

I believe in the assertions that men and women experience pain in different ways. I see no point in comparing apples to oranges, so speculation as to who can handle pain better is for overly competitive guys. Women are more highly evolved than that. It's been my experience that women are the marathon runners of pain and men are the sprinters. A man can chop his hand off at the wrist with a power saw and ask for a band-aid. A woman can endure 14 hours of labor (average for the first child) followed by 18 years of whining.

Caution: Major digression ahead.

It's funny how things can come full circle with different generations. Somehow, our generation decided that natural childbirth was the way to go. I believed the propaganda and chose to birth my babies like they did in the old days—just short of squatting in the field to drop the baby on its head. I was panting and blowing my way through the contractions so that I wouldn't lower the baby's heart rate or slow down the labor and delivery.

My mom was smoking cigarettes and taking hits of ether when she pooped me out. The drug of choice today is the epidural. You basically paralyze yourself chemically from the waist down. Aside from new advances in pharmacology and your inability to waddle outside for a cigarette after the epidural, the current labor and delivery procedure is practically the same as it was in Mom's day.

Grandma's pill shoebox
Grandma Saari took nothing but a daily vitamin for most of her life. Grandma Holt had a shoebox full of little brown bottles. I would look at her shoebox and think, wouldn't it be cool if I had to take pills from a little brown bottle? When mom explained to me the meaning of the word "hypochondria," I immediately thought of the box and started looking at the brown bottles as a one-way trip to the nut house.

If there's a phobia for becoming a hypochondriac, I've had it since that day. Unfortunately, if medications had nutritional value, I would have to call my morning routine a diet. I have rued each new bottle I've had to add to my collection ever since I stopped self-medicating with vodka. Now I'm steadily adding aging-body pills: osteoporosis, arthritis, and acid reflux. The pharmacist knows my name, birth date, shoe size, and sexual

Chapter 3

fantasies.[5] So I owe an apology to Grandma Holt. It seems that when I get all judgy, it invariably comes back to bite me in the butt.

Now I have to worry about drug interactions. When you're taking a chemical cocktail, you don't want to drive, operate heavy machinery, or take a field sobriety test. Many drugs give you dry mouth, which rarely comes up in your computer dating profile. "I like long walks on the beach, and my breath can wilt lettuce." I recently had a bad reaction to a new drug. The doctor, in all seriousness, told me to come in immediately if I experienced sudden major heart failure. I tried to picture myself driving into the clinic while having a heart attack. I've done stupider things, but usually not on doctor's orders.

With the discovery of so many new syndromes, drug companies are making a fortune on diseases of the youth challenged, and many known maladies are just now coming into the limelight. I'm not trying to trivialize anybody's health concerns. Many symptoms are severe enough to interfere with normal activities. Erectile dysfunction is the chief cause of severe cramping in the hand. Irritable bowel can force your toilet to take out a restraining order. Overactive bladder can ruin your

---

[5] An old Chevy, George Clooney, and a quart of raspberry sherbet

dreams of becoming a marathon runner or bungee jumper. Soon they'll have to come out with a drug for loss of dignity.

WebMD – God's gift to hypochondriacs

It used to be that you had a symptom, and your mom would diagnose the problem and treat it. My treatments generally included Metamucil, because my neighbor convinced Mom that regularity would cure all ills. The home remedies often bordered on the bizarre. My grandmother rubbed a slice of onion on my nose to get rid of warts. With onion juice coating my nose and irritating my eyes, all I could do was hope for multiple fire ant bites to ease my suffering. Mom made a poultice of meat tenderizer for bee stings. Try to look cool while walking around with a soggy lump of seasoning on your head.

Yes, Mom was the first line of defense against all childhood ills, but personally, I figure she had to be making some of those remedies up. She swore by an over-the-counter ointment called Nupercainal. Every cut, scrape, and bruise was treated by the wonder drug. I was 50 years old before I discovered that Nupercainal was a hemorrhoid ointment. My mother loves a good joke!

Mom had this remedy in the fridge called Coke syrup. It was exactly what it sounds like – the business

Chapter 3

end of a fountain soda. I think I can be forgiven for hedging on any number of symptoms that might get me Mom's placebo of choice. After she switched her placebo of choice to cod liver oil and an enema, I was cured!

Later generations of mothers (myself included) would cool their heels in the doctor's waiting room for every runny nose and rash on their little ones. Once, my daughter was screaming in pain. I rushed her in for an emergency appendectomy, only to find out it was gas.

Having an overactive imagination was no easy task. I was a Navy wife, and in my early dealings with the military medical system, you could honestly wait on hold for 45 minutes just to get an appointment. Taking my child to the doctor's every time symptoms presented as flatulence or toe fungus required grit, determination, and a fatalistic outlook.

Now we have the option of WebMD, the magical ether in which tiny leprechaun doctors reside. It's the first place to go if you believe a computer can accurately pinpoint your illness without the benefit of lab work or medical training. With WebMD mothers can once again make a diagnosis from the comfort of their own homes. Does your child have a cough? Look up tuberculosis on the internet. Not sure? Click on the "symptom finder". If that doesn't scare you, you just aren't doing enough research.

WebMD allows you to read articles on sleep apnea or hair replacement. Learn more about arthritis, diabetes, and head lice. After all is said and done, it often comes right back down to regularity. Mom was ahead of her time. I wonder how many children are chugging Metamucil as we speak?

Name that symptom
I recently had a Tarot reading in which I was told that illness was in my future and not to ignore any symptoms, no matter how small. Oh, boy! That opens the door to one of my favorite games – "Which symptom is going to kill me?"

Will the empty sensation in my chest be lung cancer, or are the headaches due to a tumor? Is the pain in my left shoulder a silent heart attack? And why do doctors even tell you about the existence of silent heart attacks? Will it help you recognize one, or to take steps to avoid one? No! The point is you won't see it coming, but you will help pay for the doctor's yacht by running in each time you feel an odd flutter.

Me: "I think I've been having repeated silent heart attacks."

Doctor: "What makes you think so?"

Me: "Because I feel fine. How long do I have?"

Chapter 3

Remember the adage, "A little knowledge is a dangerous thing?" It applies tenfold to hypochondria. Oh, why did I have to learn one of the symptoms of the bubonic plague is a rash? It only stands to reason the ticks that carry Lyme disease are so small they're barely visible. I could have deer ticks all over me as we speak and not know it. Then if I get a bulls-eye rash, how can I be sure it's not the plague? Perhaps we should wrap ourselves in a cocoon of ignorance, happily going through life thinking shingles are just something you put on your roof.

The truly amazing thing is that we can function at all, when you consider the complexity of all the internal systems that must work together in order to keep us walking and talking. Looking at what a miracle life is, I have every reason to be a glass half-full kind of girl where my health is concerned. I just don't have the ability.

If you have an erection lasting more than four hours, call your doctor
In the early days of prescription drug advertising, the FCC would not allow the mention of the actual illness on the commercial. So you would have to guess the disease for which the drug was designed. Let me see, do I have:

Aching in my arms, legs or neck?

Bad breath?
Gas and bloating?
Thoughts of apple pie?
Nose hair?
Irregularly shaped toenails?

If you answered yes to any of the symptoms above, ask your doctor about Speufar.

I often wondered if people actually ran to their doctors asking if Speufar was right for them when they had no idea what condition it treated. If you sounded out the name of the aforementioned pretend drug, you'll realize I still sometimes have third-grade potty humor.

The best part of any drug commercial is the disclaimer.

"Speufar should not be taken by infants, lab rats, bikers, or the criminally insane. Do not take Speufar prior to sky diving, getting married, committing suicide, or operating heavy equipment. Stop taking Speufar and seek medical help immediately if you experience ringing in your ears, vomiting, numbness in hands or feet, amnesia, embolism, sudden increase in ear wax, or the onset of Tourette's syndrome."

Now that drug companies can advertise diseases to go with the drug names, we can have a disorder or syndrome for everybody. Bring on your restless legs; you

Chapter 3

can twitch all the way to the bank to take out a second mortgage for the meds.

I'm thinking that the next step is for them to create a new designer disease. Then they can come up with the drug guaranteed to cure me of Sudden Kerosene Inhalant Disorder (SKID). Symptoms include dizziness, slurred speech, and pooping your pants.

Send in the rodeo clowns
A funny thing happened to me on the way to menopause; I became a fan of professional bull riding. As if that weren't enough, I bought a musty smelling, second-hand snakeskin and suede western jacket – WITH FRINGE. Did I mention it is dyed forest green and has long dangling laces at the cuffs with heavy miniature musket balls attached to the ends? Each time I reach up to brush the hair out of my eyes, these decorative yo-yos from hell swing away from my body, gathering speed before arcing back to bludgeon me in the face. Not everyone can pull off that look.

I'm pretty sure hormones are involved, because the same time I began listening to Tim McGraw, I lost all desire for chocolate. I bought a jeep and tuned my radio to WEZL, "the weasel," for the best in country music, and the worst in names for a radio station. At this point, my family started gearing up for an intervention. I agreed to go only if they had a bluegrass band and a hayride.

I saw no mention of this in the brochures at the doctor's office. I think there should be some kind of warning that the symptoms of menopause include hot flashes, irritability, weight gain, night sweats, and a desire to visit Dollywood.

I decided to run with it and paid top dollar for the best seats when the PBR (Professional Bull Riding) tour came to town. As the cowboys were introduced, I cheered and clapped, smacking myself repeatedly with my jacket laces. We were in the front row, right next to the gates. From this distance, I could see every acne scar on the faces of the kids riding thousands of pounds of angry pot roast. The cowboys didn't look old enough to shave, and the lineup included one Amish lad on his Rumspringa.[6] Can you imagine? After living a simple life for sixteen years, you're given a year to go nuts and you choose serial trampling over Jäger?

Soon I found myself staring into the bloodshot eyes of a huge white Brahma bull, with only two feet and a flimsy rail separating us. It seemed to be fixated on my green jacket. It stood staring long enough to give me plenty of time to reconsider my recent fashion decisions.

---

[6] An Amish rite of passage, characterized by debauchery, hedonism, and an arrest tecord.

Chapter 3

When he finally returned to the chutes I had made up my mind – I'll cancel the line dancing lessons.

I don't know where this mid-life affinity for all things country will take me. I only know that when I get there, I'll smell like Grandma's attic and have tiny pellet sized bruises on my face.

Preschool panic

Chickenpox, and head lice. If you missed out on any of these when your children were in school, fate has given you a second chance by way of grandchildren. Before you realize a child is sick, he has already shared the condition with every other child at his designer, exclusive preschool. When *your* grandchild brings chickenpox home from his government-subsidized preschool, be prepared to babysit for weeks. Junior is going to spread the disease to every other junior and juniorette in the family. If you haven't had chickenpox already, prepare to buy out all the calamine lotion in your local drugstore.

While you can't recognize chickenpox in time to prevent its spread, you don't want to recognize head lice. No matter how many kids are walking around with nits on their noodle, if you're the first one to report it your child is viewed as the instigator. Other parents look at you with scorn as they wait at the checkout with their lice shampoo. They should be thanking you for raising the alarm. No good deed goes unpunished. If you want to be censured and mocked, please look for these typical lice warning signs:

- The presence of white rice-like eggs attached to the hairs
- Excessive scratching of the scalp
- Little bugs dancing around like Mexican jumping beans
- All the other kids at the school wearing hats.

Don't sweat the small stuff

I've never been to an Indian sweat lodge, but I know they are believed to provide physical and spiritual benefits. The Finnish equivalent provides physical stimulation and bragging rights. You don't see any self-respecting Native American beating himself with an alder switch in the sauna, then stepping out and diving straight into an icy lake (and I say this with all due respect to my Finnish relations), because it's nuts!

My personal trainer on a video workout said the better shape you're in, the faster you break a sweat. He had a long well thought-out explanation, but it kind of flew in the face of the truisms from my childhood.

Mom: "He can bench press an engine block without breaking a sweat, but he can't put down a toilet seat!"

Chapter 3

Sweat has the desired effect of removing toxins from your body. It has the undesired effect of removing people from your vicinity.

"Gee, Karla. It looks like you've been doing yard work in the hot sun all day!" My friend exclaimed.

"Yes, I guess I got a little sunburned."

"Well, you look a little sticky and uncomfortable. Would you like a glass of lemonade and a bar of soap?"

"Actually, I'm starving. How does sushi sound to you?"

My friend shook her head. "Why don't we stay here and eat on the patio. Which way is the wind blowing?"

My dirty little secret: I haven't used antiperspirant in years. I opted for deodorant because I didn't want to *not* sweat: I just didn't want to stink while sweating. Since the onset of hot flashes had me sweating faster than I could shower or deodorize, I am re-thinking any suspected health risks that might be related to antiperspirant. I'm tired of sitting on the loveseat of loneliness in a crowded room.

Toilet Seat Cooties

Since the invention of the modern valve and siphon flush toilet by Thomas Crapper (1837-1910), the water closet has been the butt of undeserved humor and derision. American soldiers returning from England after WWI first linked Tom's good name with the bad contents of said toilet. It's unclear as to when rejoicing over this boon to sanitation turned into paranoia and conspiracy theories, connected with the toilet part that we connect with. Some give credit to Crapper's mother-in-law.

"Look Ethel. You'll never have to use a chamber pot again!" Tom crooned. "The flush toilet gets rid of 95% more of what you want to get rid of."

"Did you already sit on this, Tom? Because there is no way I am going to share your cooties!"

"It's perfectly sanitary."

"You couldn't have invented paper toilet seat covers while you were at it? I could be sitting here, minding my own business while staff, boils, warts, or syphilis are dancing around beneath me."

"I don't have syphilis, Ethel!"

"And would it kill you to put the toilet seat down when you're finished?"

Since then, those who swear they face the imminent danger of "death by public restroom" have developed several coping mechanisms for avoiding other people's bacteria. If there are no paper toilet seat covers, they will use toilet paper to line the cover. There are danglers, who hover over the toilet, splashing their own goodies on the seat as a gift for the next person. Danglers would crawl over their spouse to escape a burning building.

Chapter 3

There are even some who carry their own cleaning products wherever they go. The Lysol spray crowd is one of the many reasons women must wait for hours in line for public restrooms. We're all waiting for Janet Hillstrom's toilet seat to dry.

Personally, I'm an adrenaline junkie. I dive right in, heedless of possible flesh eating bacteria left by Jane O'CeeDee. By the way, Jane, you should probably go to the doctor and get that checked out.

Well meaning advice from friends
Medical experts agree that the treatment for your rash should not be loudly debated on the subway or at the office water cooler. There is, however, no ethical requirement for confidentiality among friends and family. Well, at least that's true among *my* friends and family. When you let the general public participate in your diagnosis, you'll find most advice you receive is based on anecdotal evidence.

"Aunt Mildred swears you should treat lumbago by bathing in salad oil. She got the idea from a radio talk show, so it must be true."

Please do not try this at home, as you will be too slippery afterward to crawl out of the bathtub without cracking your skull. If you try it anyway, you never heard it from Aunt Mildred.

Most free advice is passed along under the heading of "they say…" Even with amazing books and internet resources; more often than not, we blindly accept recommendations based on this dubious endorsement. The good news is that "they" are often right. I don't know of any physical condition unique to just one human. There is a certain sense of comfort in knowing that whatever you are going through, there is a "they" out there who has been through it as well, and understands.

My youngest daughter is the medical expert in our family. Not only has she done extensive muscular system study for massage therapy, she was also a veterinary technician for many years. If I pull a muscle or get heartworms, she is my go-to girl.

I used to belly dance for fun (honestly) but if I did a Turkish Drop today, you'd have to pry me off the floor with a spatula. I can't even hold my arms up long enough to blow-dry my hair. I should count myself lucky that most of my health concerns are the normal aches and pains of getting old. In spite of all the negatives, hypochondria can also have its advantages. Do you know what the best part of all the obsessing and complaining is? Sometimes I can be a "they" for somebody else.

Chapter 4
Burden to your Children

Opportunities to impose on your progeny are limited only by your imagination. From using them as a designated golf cart driver after a wild night of Canasta and debauchery, to expecting them to change your diaper, you can make "eldercare" a dirty word in their vocabulary. Of course, in hard economic times, you might have to move in with them or camp out in their backyard. Hopefully, your kids will respond to guilt trips when you need something from them, because mine won't.

Timing is everything

When I was young, I would wait expectantly day after day for the prize patrol to knock on our door. Each summer, when I visited my grandparents, I donated huge DNA samples, licking and pasting magazine stamps into blank boxes. I put secret prize stickers into hidden envelopes and watched grandpa package up the whole gloppy mess to send to "Sweepstakes Central." Every year when they announced the winner, it turned out to be some octogenarian in Omaha (town motto: The contest is fixed). The winner received his prize of a jillion dollars in the form of an annuity payment of $150,000 per year for both of the remaining years of his life.

Even as a kid I suspected something was fishy. Could any one demographic be that lucky? Perhaps only seniors had free hours (eight and a half) to spend perforating, licking, and sticking their way to financial independence. Perhaps dinosaurs still roam the earth in North Dakota, just outside of Bismarck.

I've worked in pension administration, where actuaries use mortality tables to figure out how many years it will take you to go from retired to buried. The other day, I overheard a senior at a restaurant saying that if you make it to 70, you'll make it to 90. I have to assume this is based on anecdotal evidence rather than actuarial equivalencies.

Your children were a burden to you for 18 to 22 years (unless they are currently living in your basement). As life expectancies increase, we may have the opportunity to be burdens to our children longer than that. Since none of us is likely to win the magazine company sweepstakes, pace yourselves!

Chapter 4

The Waltons

In an agrarian society, the practice in the past was to have extended families living together. Families had to be large enough for the children to have a bigger base and better odds when drawing straws for supporting Mom and Dad. When short straw junior took over the farm, parents, grandparents, and appliances would convey with the house.

You would think siblings would be eager to pursue their dreams, while the unlucky heir was tied to farm and family. Aside from John Boy's dreams of becoming a journalist, it was not so on the TV show, The Waltons. Villagers could come with torches and pitchforks, but nothing short of an actors' strike would budge the Walton children from their mountain.

By contrast, in an industrial society, most families today average 2½ children. The chance of extended families living together is preempted by alarm systems, deadbolts, and razor wire. That still does not absolve children of the responsibility for their aging parents. Since the odds of drawing the short straw on senior care increase sharply as brood size drops off, the retirement home starts looking very attractive to your 2½ kids.

"Good night, Nurse Susan."

Drunken party grandma

Every family has one … the party girl who can swear like a sailor, hold more liquor than a bar, and stay up until the cows come home. Back in the day I could do all the above without breaking a sweat. (OK. I didn't have a potty mouth.) My grandmother never touched a drop of alcohol, because that's how the Pentecostals roll. I'll bet my grandmother never dreamt of belly dancing in a bar in downtown Seattle. I did, because that's how the Episcopalians roll.

I have since given up on my dream of being the family black sheep, so my mother has had to step into the breach to become the current reigning party grandma in our family.

My youngest daughter (code name: Chiclet) leads the most sober and boring lifestyle of anyone in our family. Mostly, she's too poor to party. Her grandmother generally does not drink grapefruit juice without vodka in it (who would?), and is the life of the party at the community center. After a busy night of playing "Poop On Your Neighbor," she wheels around the neighborhood in her golf cart, flashing her ample bosom at the Anderson twins, Herb and Frank. When other grandmothers are going to prayer meetings and baking pies for the Post 13 VFW carnival and white elephant sale, my mother is loudly asking Mabel Gunderson to go

Chapter 4

to the bingo hall bathroom with her and make sure that she doesn't fall off the pot.

If Chiclet lived near my mother, she might be called upon to take over the golf cart on Friday nights in a twisted version of Driving Miss Crazy.

"I hear the Sonoma County Harvest Festival features vintners from all up and down the Napa Valley. I think I'll go there next Sunday for the wine tasting." Mom remarked.

"The golf cart is not approved for public roads, Grandma."

"How about if we get a keg and invite the water aerobic class to a bonfire by the river? After a couple shots of vodka, I can do the limbo."

"After a couple shots of vodka you'll be lucky to get your support hose off."

"It's ladies' night at the Salty Poopdeck. I could wear my spandex mini skirt."

"Grandma, just give me the keys so you'll have both hands free to flash the Anderson brothers."

It just goes to show you're never too old to be an embarrassment to your grandchildren.

Could you reach that for me?
When I was in Kindergarten, we were forced to perform the movements to the song, "Head and Shoulders; Knees

and Toes." When Grandma first told me this was a staple for exercise sessions at her assisted living center, I: a) made fun of a group of people too immobile to do the Hokey Pokey, and; b) went into a panic. I should have paid more attention when they taught us the song in kindergarten.

You can probably guess the outcome. Like some kind of cosmic thirty-year Karma, my mocking has come back to haunt me. I have degenerative disk disease in my neck. Now it's all I can do to keep my arms up long enough to wash my hair. Since it hurts to run the vacuum, dust bunnies are making baby dust bunnies and are taking over the house.

I have a little concern about the effect of physical limitations on cleanliness. I've been in several homes that have a distinctive old person odor. I suspect the funk is due to the inability of seniors to reach down far enough to wash in between their toes. I have recently noticed a hint of this aroma in my closet, which leads me to thank God no intruder has felt it necessary to break in and try on my middle age sundress collection. How embarrassing would that be?

As long as the old-people smell stays confined to the closet, I won't have to ask my kids to help me clean house. I'll save calling in that favor for when I can no longer perform Head and Shoulders; Knees and Toes.

Chapter 4

Guard Duty

My great aunt and uncle disappeared out of the blue one day. When their children tried to find them, they learned that Mom and Dad's last known location was at a small carnival. I can't say if they met with foul play or ran away from home to join the circus. Since I only knew one of Dad's cousins well, I don't feel qualified to make any totally unjustified and inconsiderate cracks about Great Aunt and Uncle trying to get away from their kids.

Nevertheless, I think it would be ill advised not to prepare for such an eventuality in your own family.

Have your kids suggested going to the vets to have you chipped? As long as my barcode isn't the number 666, I see nothing wrong with the idea. It's just when they start pinning my name and address to my shirt that I'll feel the first twinges of panic. My kids want me to have the illusion of freedom, so they've offered to put in an electric fence and have me outfitted with a very smart and classy looking shock collar. I asked that they get it in red, since that is my power color.

If I go on a trip, my daughter insists I call to let her know I arrived safely. It's very sweet of her, but I often turn off my phone and forget to call. She's got a notebook filled with phone numbers for sheriff's offices and hospital emergency rooms in areas we've frequented. I'm pretty convinced that if we ever tried to run away, she could track us down. New advances like OnStar and GPS tracking make it very unlikely I'll ever work the Midway in the Globfarts Traveling Circus. Upside, I'll be safe from evil, creepy looking clowns.

Diaper doody
My children have proclaimed that when my husband and I get old, they will care for us. Then they immediately cough while saying "nursing home" under their breath. When Pampers were still a novelty, I was doing diaper duty with cloth diapers. My husband was out to sea most of the time, so it was usually me looking down the business end of baby orifices. I totally blame my mom for my persistence in rejecting disposable diapers. When she was a newlywed, Mom's washing machine was a galvanized washtub and a washboard; her dryer was a clothesline. She washed my diapers in boiling water and proudly claimed I had the cleanest diapers in town. I naturally wanted to emulate my mom, laundry OCD and all. At least I skipped the washtub and clothesline.

Sure, I could have legitimately played the "too poor for disposables" card, but I went instead with the self righteous "cloth diapers breathe and are better for sensitive skin" approach. Meanwhile, I used industrial strength laundry detergent and bleach instead of a gentle

Chapter 4

laundry soap, I folded the diapers so that they were bulky in all the wrong places, and occasionally poked the baby with diaper pins.

My oldest daughter, who won a full scholarship to a prestigious women's college in Baltimore, took four years to learn how to use big girl panties. She was not a potty seat prodigy. While she may be embarrassed that I shared that little piece of family lore, it won't equal my humiliation when asking her to change my diaper.

Me: "I'm feeling a little funky and my sciatica is burying the pain needle each time I reach below my waist. Do you think you could please give me a hand with … you know?"

Daughter: "Mom, I changed your diaper yesterday, and Dad asked me first. No line jumping."

Me: "I didn't make you wait during all those four years of childhood incontinence. You were always changed so promptly you never suffered a single day of diaper rash. I had to rinse poopy diapers in the toilet so I wouldn't contribute to the landfill – and I never complained."

Daughter: "The guilt card didn't work when I was ten. What makes you think it's going to work now?"

Me: "Don't make me get my smacking glove!"

When I get to that point, I hope my kids spring for disposable diapers. Bleach irritates my sensitive skin, and I'm not sure they even make diaper pins anymore.

Purse strings politics

Besides being an incontinent social burden to our children, I think we must address the elephant in the room ... money. If by some miracle the Social Security System lives longer than we do, we may find ourselves on a fixed income. That used to be the bad news. Now we keep our fingers crossed that before we shuffle off this mortal coil, there still is an income to fix. The alternative falls to either moving in with one of our 2½ children or being adopted by a pack of wolves.

Since wolves tend to kill and eat their elders, it will probably be your children who take you in. This is where all your parenting sins will catch up to you. Did you make your kids wear saddle shoes?[7] Prepare for orthopedic socks and underwear next Christmas. Did you make your kids eat brussels sprouts? You can expect a diet of fat-free, salt-free, sugar-free, taste-free food. Junior will quickly find that holding the purse strings is the best revenge!

---

[7] Shoes made with leather so ugly, the cow was glad to part with it.

Chapter 4

It's too late to have regrets over the times you were tough but fair with your kids. Those excellent values you taught them are the reason they feel compassion, and they care enough to put up with you. Every privilege you made them earn, every bad thing you denied them was for their own good. Still, it blows when they tell you the chicken liver casserole is for your own good. I bet you wish you had let them keep that stray kitten now.

We want to be independent and self sufficient for as long as possible. Each thing we lose: our energy, our mobility, our teeth; represents a chapter closing in our lives. When moving in with children, hopefully, we will find a way to make ourselves feel useful. We don't want to give them an excuse to kill and eat their elders.

What's the word I'm looking for?
I've never been good at stringing coherent sentences together, which leads one to wonder why I'm writing a book. More and more, my children have to fill in the conversational blanks when my voice trails away mid-thought. My family and friends know me well enough to finish my sentences, but it is frequently my kids who have the responsibility of being my interpreter. Fortunately, they are fluent in dementia.

I like to think my train of thought is an express, so it misses a few stops along the way. That sounds better than saying my verbal skills died an untimely death about the time I started growing a mustache. When I fall into a conversational black hole, I don't fill in the blanks gracefully. Unintelligible sounds ooze out of me as if I just woke up in Tijuana, after drinking tequila all night with a goat and two chickens.

Besides having too many words on the tip of my tongue and not enough in my head, I am several beats behind in any conversation. I've always wanted to be a sharp-witted "pistol" during discussions. More often than not, I tend to be a "blunderbuss".

Son: "I heard that maple doughnuts have been found to cause cancer in lab rats."

Daughter: "That's only if they use the artificial maple flavoring."

Son: "Doesn't real maple flavoring have high alcohol content, just like vanilla extract? Do you think that would kill any carcinogens?"

Daughter: "I don't think so. You don't hear of a lower incidence of cancer in alcoholics."

Son: "That wouldn't be a reliable statistic because alcoholics will drink anything from gasoline to mouthwash."

Daughter: "You'd have to be pretty messed up to drink gasoline!"

Me: "I like maple doughnuts."

Chapter 4

I generally find that the word or name I'm looking for occurs to me as I'm going to bed, or when I'm sitting on the toilet. I recommend keeping a handy spiral bound notebook in the bathroom to jot down your thoughts for mental hiccup emergencies later. For example:

Larry Hagman played J.R. Ewing in Dallas and that Air Force Major in I Dream of Jeannie. What's that character's name?

A drawer full of scarves
My grandma was obsessed with keeping us warm when I was little. She had a collection of red wool huivis[8] which she forced us to wear when we went out to play. I felt sorry for myself because I looked like a dork. I also felt sorry for the poor sheep that produced this wool. If it was chafing torture for me to have it tied under my chin, imagine how it must have been for the creature who had to wear coarse grit sandpaper all over his body.

Nothing says "slit your writs and be done with it" to me like shopping. When my grandmother got a studio apartment in a retirement home, I was faced with the dilemma of finding the gift that takes up no space. At my best, I am a very poor Christmas shopper. I walk out of a store with six gifts for myself, and a candle. Perhaps it's the huivi trauma I suffered as a child, but each year, the

---

[8] Finnish for truly hideous scarves

only gift I could come up with for grandma was a scarf. She had a drawer full of huivis she never wore.

Stop whining, grandma! Mom had to put up with a drawer full of aprons.

Now I conscript my daughter into being my personal shopper. She finds and wraps all my gifts, and helps me when I hyperventilate in the mall. Eventually, I'll get her a headset so I can monitor the operation from command central. I'll be eating raspberry sherbet in my pajamas while she gets into a fistfight with a roller derby jammer over the last Play Station.

Left to my own devices, I once gave my son a hydraulic jack, just because he likes car stuff, and I don't remember the reasoning that went into buying my daughter a blanket rack. When my son took a stab at being my personal shopper, I passed gas in the tool section. It smelled like a herd of water buffalo had been loosed in the hammer aisle. I had defiled the most sacred area of the department store, and my son was horrified that the salesmen would think it was him. He hasn't been back to that store since.

Now that I've moved into a smaller house, I have no room for dust catchers on my shelves, or in my garage, so my kids are faced with the drama of shopping for me. The choice is perfectly clear: either put up with my funk because the two microwaves and a food processor they

Chapter 4

bought me are stored in my bathtub; or buy something small I can stash neatly in the back of my underwear drawer (behind the granny panties and industrial strength Wonder Bras). I imagine it's only a matter of time before they start adding a splash of color to my wardrobe, rescuing me from my own attempts at accessorizing. If they are reading this I hope they remember not to get a scarf with orange in it. Fall colors make me look like I ate undercooked pork.

Sick and tired
"I'm wondering if I should have that laser corrective eye surgery," my neighbor, Irene said. "I'm tired of dealing with glasses."

"I hear you," I agreed. "I'm tired of having to deal with my prosthetic arm. It's a pain when I misplace it."

"Yeah, I'm sick of having to get a new crown every year," she said. "I'm pouring a fortune into my teeth."

"Tell me about it! I just paid three and a half thousand bucks for a partial."

She tried again. "I hear there's a new medication out for migraines. I get them about twice a month, and would welcome some relief."

"The doctors are pretty sure they got all the brain tumor when I had surgery last year, but I still get headaches … I mean, now that I'm out of the coma and all."

"Oh well," she sighed. "At least I have a kidney transplant donor so I can get off dialysis."

"I'm so happy to hear that!" I enthused. "Maybe we can share a hospital room when I go in for my heart, lung, liver, and pancreas transplant."

"Mom, you are such a liar!" My daughter growled. "You know you're only getting a heart, lung and liver." She turned to my neighbor. "Believe me, Irene, you do not want to be around her whiny ass when she's recovering from surgery. I'm sick and tired of having to nurse her through another three days of hell!"

Reality check
While we are complaining about losing our driving privileges after backing over a gas pump (I'm pretty sure I had right of way), our kids are saddled with the extra responsibility of providing us with transportation. I'm a glass half-empty kind of girl. Age can gradually strip a person of strength, health, and dignity. I hope that as I get older, I can spend more time in gratitude for what I have than in self-pity for what I've lost. No promises.

In the current economy, many of our children are faced with caring for their parents, at the same time as having to care for their own grown children. Be careful to

Chapter 4

watch for telltale signs of stress. Do they argue about money? Do they have a police scanner to keep track of their kids? Do they have Dr. Kavorkian on speed dial, to take care of their parents?

I've taught my kids that in situations such as this, if you don't laugh you're going to cry. That is why I get the evil mad scientist laugh any time my kids and I talk about the subject of adult care. "Bwa ha ha!"

(Long pause) I Dream of Jeannie ... Major Nelson!

Chapter 5
Mid-life Madness

Now is the time to take stock of missed mid-life crisis opportunities. Sure you got a tattoo, but now you need a Harley to go with it. If you can't afford a cool bike, at least get the leather chaps. Hurry and take that white water rafting trip, before your bones become brittle enough to crack in a strong wind. Don't forget your drastic and costly career change. My well thought-out choice was to become a poverty-stricken writer. The urgency is that you need to hurry and finish your mid-life crisis before you can get started working on your bucket list.

Shake your booty

For a couple of years running, my kids attended an annual rock festival. This event featured multiple big name bands and tens of thousands of young people attending raves, line jumping, and littering. To ensure my children did not participate in such debauchery, I attended these concerts in a chaperone capacity. One

Chapter 5

year, my stable influence included getting my nipple pierced.

I'll never know what insanity took me, but I found myself in a vending stall with three college girls and a nun, all of us subjecting intimate parts to the needle. When I told my kids I was going to get pierced after lunch, four of the young men accompanying us asked if they could watch.

"I don't know, guys. Post-lunch timing might be a problem. Once you take one look at my far from perky middle age breast, you might be spewing hot dogs and elephant ears. You probably don't want front row seats."

Fortunately, that decision was taken out of my hands by a "one person only" audience rule. In the end, it was only my oldest daughter holding my hand.

"Mom, I'm so proud of you. All through that, you didn't scream once!"

"Sweetie, I was screaming from the moment I saw the clamp, but it was a noise that only dogs could hear."

Afterwards, I tried to be discreet. I didn't want to expose my temporary insanity to any of my stable accountant coworkers. This is why you should never bring your children with you to company social events. The same daughter who was proud of me for not screaming informed me in a loud voice that the ball on my nipple ring was poking through my bra.

Clearly, the cat was out of the bag, with no graceful way to get it back in. My office posse had already caught glimpses of my tattoo when I wore strappy tops. (No, it was not on my butt. Don't believe everything you hear.) Accountants see the world as an equation.

Tattoo = biker babe.

Tattoo + nipple ring = the Anti-Christ.

If that were true, then satanic, baby-eating anarchists don't pee in the sink or pick their noses in public. Who knew?

I missed all the fun

The tattoo and nipple ring notwithstanding, I must have been taking a nap when my midlife crisis passed by. I didn't buy my 1954 Thunderbird or my cherry red women's Harley. I should have learned ballroom dancing, traveled the lake country of Estonia, or opened a bed and breakfast in Boise, Idaho. I thought events of that nature defined a mid-life crisis.

Reassess your goals if you must, but what I wanted was to do things that were totally out of character. My personality is defined more than anything else by my inability to break rules. I could no more shoplift a candy bar than I could milk a pig[9].

---

[9] No pigs were harmed in the making of this analogy

Chapter 5

So I expected mid-life would be full of daring-do and naughtiness. I could have:
- Trespassed on private property
- Peed in the pool
- Tipped cows in the middle of the night
- Worn white shoes after labor day.

Instead, I swapped husbands, jobs, and churches, like they were cookie recipes, and survived five of the ten most stressful life events (according to a popular women's magazine). While others were sipping Mai Tais in Hawaii, my forties and fifties were all about the fastest way to get an ulcer.

I would have preferred mid-life to be all about the sexy car.

The theory of relativity

I've never seen a picture of Albert Einstein as a young man. He's always pictured as old, with white hair in a style that makes a llama on a windy day look well groomed by comparison. So it comes as no surprise to me that Einstein was the father of the theory of relativity. I see his theory as the observation that time is speeding up as I get older. Einstein was obviously working on the theory for at least two hundred years, but it felt like only fifty.

When we were babies, our parents counted our ages in weeks, then months. As we got older, we made a point of adding "and a half" between birthdays. Whether I'm 678 months old or .0565^{10} light years is pretty irrelevant. I can't even keep up with changing the number once a year. I'm not too vain to admit my age, just too old to remember it.

I'm alarmed that I'm thinking of the recent past as a few decades ago rather than a few years ago. I've started measuring time by John Travolta, who was lighting up the disco dance floor in 1977, and dancing with Uma Thurman in 1994. I was so busy watching his metamorphosis of bad hairstyles in recent movies that I didn't even notice my term life insurance policy had reached its expiration date. The Mayan calendar ran out in 2012, but my blue book value bottomed out in 2009. There's something ominous about that.

While time speeds up, the novelty of life events is kissing the pavement. We certainly haven't seen it all, but we've come close. We watched Tiny Tim marry Miss Vicki on The Tonight Show. Compared to that, the sameness of even the best traditions acts like novocain to the brain. By the way, I was shocked to find out that most dentists stopped using novocain decades ago, and are now using more effective drugs like lidocaine. I feel betrayed and deceived, but I'll continue to refer to dental

Chapter 5

anesthetics as novocain. Cut me some slack; I'm old. If these trends continue, will I have anything to say in my annual Christmas letter?

"This year has been a lot like last year. I had dental work and we did stuff."

Bad hair day

Many cultures would practice cutting a maiden's long hair when she married, as a representation of the end of childhood and innocence. Long hair on senior women is reserved for biker babes, new AARP (American Association of Ripe People) candidates, Valerie Bertinelli and Marie Osmond. Both of the latter have flowing tresses and advertise diet systems. I haven't figured out the connection, but it's just a little too convenient to be coincidence.

About 85% of men[10] prefer women with long hair, so we refuse to lop our locks as long as possible when we move into womanhood. I balked at cutting my hair shorter than shoulder length because I have a very large head and head bumps so weird they once grossed out a doctor. Short hair is never a good look on a lumpy melon-head.

You can curl it, layer it, or tousle it, but no matter what you do, short hair makes you look older and less

---

[10] A wild guess.

feminine. I had often wondered, "What possessed that woman to get a Marine recruit haircut?" or, "Could she possibly put more gel on less hair?" One of the defining moments in my life was when I gave up and got the "old lady haircut". This is characterized as any cut that requires shaving the back of the neck.

The reason was simple, yet elegant. Hot flashes trump vanity. I got to where I couldn't stand any hair on my neck, and ponytails were getting pretty old. The short hair dilemma comes when it's time to touch up my roots. You can change the color, but when short, my hair will still exhibit the wiry texture of gray hair. This causes individual hairs to stick straight up or straight out. Longer hair is heavier and forces the little stragglers down, but too short and I start to look like a cactus.

The next logical step is to buy a red hat. Oh, don't tell me hairstyles are not the inspiration for the Red Hat Society. Agnes is the Sergeant at Arms for the local chapter and she guards the secret handshake from anyone with hair below chin-length.

"Well, you definitely have old lady hair, so you are guaranteed membership," Agnes said.

"Red and purple are good colors for me, and I like to get out with others. I guess I'll enlist."

"We have a handy online gift shop where you can find the most outrageously cute hats," she continued.

Chapter 5

"I wonder what style would suit me?"

"Unfortunately, you'll have to shop our special selection. We don't have many styles in lumpy melon size."

I just can't get a break.

Putting a smiley face on failure

By the time you hit mid-life, you will have let milk go bad in the refrigerator approximately 132 times. You can either lose sleep over spoiled milk and moldy cheese, or you can give yourself permission to try again. Our family has a tradition of passing around a medallion with the Celtic rune[11] of "New Beginnings."

I first bought the rune for my daughter when she was expelled from school. I got it back from her when I divorced my husband, and have been guardian of the failure rune ever since. There is the adage, "When God closes a door he opens a window," which has the same meaning as our rune. If this adage is true, God watches you fall on your face, then puts your arthritis to the test by making you climb through a window. It's like some cosmic funny home video show. I hope it's not a second or third story window! Personally, I'd rather believe in a loving God who will provide another door and maybe an elevator.

---

[11] Snotty name for symbol

Part of the human condition is the *ability* to pick ourselves up and start over when we fail. Part of my condition is the lack of *desire* to start over when I fail. Most recently, I had to quit a high stress job because I was losing sleep and having panic attacks. I dusted off the rune and gave myself the usual pep talk.

Monologue: "Edison said that if you fall on your face, at least you're heading in the right direction. As long as you've done your best, you've done enough. This is why God made chocolate."

The first step towards accepting your failures and reevaluating your life is to understand yourself. I chose to do this by journaling my dreams. The first night I dreamt I ran into the store and left my pet goldfish, Mr. Peanut, sitting in the car.

Oh, don't start on me. I cracked the window.

When I returned to the parking lot, my car was gone. I sank to my knees, and wept into a puddle of oil. Obviously, I was a terrible parent, and probably had a cracked head on my Buick.

It all comes down to this. Mid-life is a great opportunity for *you* to learn from your mistakes, take stock, reevaluate your priorities; and work toward being healthy physically, spiritually, and psychologically. It's a good opportunity for *me* to regret poor life decisions, find somebody else to blame for my problems, and wish I had a cosmetics consultant to help me find the right shade of foundation.

Go for broke

I decided I should celebrate mid-life with my first and only white water rafting trip. It's me, a hunk of plastic, and my osteoporosis against a class-five rapid. What could go wrong? So we loaded up for the New River Gorge in West Virginia. I paid for the trip in advance so I'd be less likely to chicken out.

My first tidbit of advice: don't bow to peer pressure when your peers are barely of legal drinking age. I can hear my mother: "If everybody jumped off a cliff, would you do it too?" Actually, Mom, it was "Jumpers' Rock" and yes, I did it too.

Our outfit had smaller boats than most, so I was within easy reach of people falling out. I made failed and half-hearted attempts to get them on the way down, and don't know what I would have done next if some part of their anatomy ended up in my hand.

"Surfing" in white water rafting is like walking up a down escalator. Our boat held its position shooting the tube of Nosebleed Drop for a new world record. I can remember reaching out to one of my shipmates in slow motion and holding his shoulder comfortingly after his girlfriend clocked him in the eye with her paddle. I continued to reach out to each of our other barely-of-age rafters to whisper words of encouragement when they began to look truly frightened. If the ordeal had been any longer, I would have made them milk and cookies.

Once a mom, always a mom.

Bathroom bar
In Spain, every ice cream shop and drug store had a bar. The walls in most establishments were covered in tile or marble: elegant, but an acoustical nightmare. Every dropped fork or whispered conversation reverberated around the room. Behind the bar (or ice cream display case, candy rack, and so forth) were glass shelves mounted to the tile wall, on which bottles of liquor were majestically perched. The contrast between the tile and the colorful glass bottles on the shelves was breathtaking.

The first time I had a bathroom with tile on the walls, I was reminded of Spain. Can you imagine what guests would think when they use the bathroom if I had gone with a Spanish decorating theme?

"Your bathroom décor is rather unusual. Where did you get the idea?"

"Isn't it cool?" I could reply. "I love the way the gold veins in the tiles go with the amber of the scotch. And the reflection of the vanity lights off the dark rum is like Jan

Chapter 5

Vermeer's use of light in his 1665 *Allegory of the Art of Painting*."

"You know, Karla, if you can't even poop without taking a drink, it may be time for some professional intervention. They have twelve-step programs for that—well not the pooping part."

"Are you saying I should have gone with a floral theme?"

Flight of fancy aside, the kind of bar I'm talking about is found on the walls of bathtubs in assisted living centers—the kind Grandpa used after his stroke. You know you're sliding down the other side of middle age when you wish you had a handlebar in your bathtub.

I've considered the super suction safety bar because of my fear of commitment. But eventually, I'll be faced with the reality of finding a couple of studs and bolting a permanent fixture to the wall. Maybe we could pass it off as a standard feature when we had the house built, or since we don't have a storm cellar, a tornado precaution. Never mind that we don't live anywhere near tornado alley.

However we choose to justify an appliance on our bathroom wall, the humiliation is a small price to pay for skeletal system integrity. I'm going with the tornado story. You'll have to come up with your own.

Packing heat

My first grown-up job was assistant dog groomer. I had to give it up because I was too slow to make any money, and I would come home with prickly hairs stuck down inside my shirt. If I'm going to feel prickly hairs against my chest, they better be attached to Sean Connery. Since then, I've had careers I thought would last forever, but which died slow and painful deaths.

For my ultimate midlife crisis, I decided to quit my job and write a book. Family and friends have appreciated my irreverent annual Christmas letters over the years, so I figured I was qualified for the position.

Not being content to simply make everything up off the top of my head, I decided I should experience first hand the action and adventure, as long as it didn't involve heavy lifting. This was the inspiration for a trip to a small town in South Carolina to search for an eight-foot lizard man living in a local swamp. Since the name "Godzilla" is already taken, we'll call him Hal. This particular reptilian hybrid likes to beat up on unsuspecting SUVs, so my son and I laid a trap using my truck as bait. We climbed up a deer blind built about the time of the revolutionary war and waited. After five minutes, Hal was a no-show and we were getting cold. It was still better than waiting in line at the post office.

Chapter 5

My next book will be a mystery, so my latest "research" involved a gun range, a .22 and the big toe on my right foot. The crater two centimeters from my shoe was surprisingly large for a small caliber rifle. In consideration of the rest of my body parts and those of my neighbors, I cut the target practice short.

I could use some practice on my lock-picking skills and I'll need a research consultant from the south end of town to teach me the finer points of hot-wiring a car. I believe I owe it to my new craft and hypothetical readers to bring realism into my stories. In the future, I'll just have to use murder weapons that don't require small ordinance in my books.

There's a hole in my bucket list
There are so many things I haven't done yet. When my son was talking about driving a bulldozer at work, I actually felt a pang of regret. Would I drive a bulldozer if I got the opportunity?

Hell, yeah!

Who wouldn't want to feel the rumble of about 2,000 horsepower and the absolute supremacy of being able to move huge chunks of the earth's crust with ease? I would even be OK with moving huge chunks of manure if it meant driving a rig with treads instead of tires. A bucket in the rear would be awesome, but I'm willing to negotiate on that one.

The more important and realistic question is, "When should I start panicking over all life's missed opportunities?" When I was a Navy wife, we always waited until the last two weeks of a tour of duty to see all the sights and take in the local atmosphere. The recent interest in a "bucket list" is a salute to all the procrastinators out there.

Since we have no idea when our tour of duty on earth ends, the wisdom is to live each day as if it was our last. It may sound like a bunch of feel-good psychobabble poop, (pardon my French) but the idea may just have some merit.

Retirement is the ultimate procrastination. It is that long awaited playground after years of hard work. Unfortunately, it is also the time when we can't stay awake for the late night news. If the Capital Building catches fire after 6:00 PM, it will just have to wait until tomorrow.

Since my procrastinating skills are epic, I feel I haven't lived my mid-life crisis to the fullest. I'll probably just defer the rest of it until I hit my 80's[12], because that's

---

[12] Remember, if you make it to 70, you'll make it to 90 according to an unimpeachable source—two guys at the Huddle House.

Chapter 5

the way I roll. By then, in the interest of finding something I haven't done before, I may have to substitute "crawdad racing" for "bungee jumping" on my bucket list. If nothing else, running the crawdad circuit will get me out to every vacation Mecca in the U.S. and Canada. I can give you the number of my bookie if you'd like a piece of the action.

Chapter 6
I wish I looked like Susan Lucci

For those people with enough money and motivation, there is no need to look like Octogenarian Barbie (now available at online retailers everywhere). The rest of us have infomercials. For three monthly payments of $39.95 plus shipping and handling, if you order in the next thirty minutes, you too can own an anti-aging serum made with rare ant vomit extract imported from Walla Walla, Washington. You may reach the point where you have to decide whether to have cosmetic surgery or try to rock the Marlon Brando jowls. Laser off those skin tags, or stay at home in your bathrobe all day with the lights turned low. The choice is up to you.

All my soap operas
In spite of short legs, a few too many pounds, and a big head, I am vain. There's no point in denying it or pretending I'm window-shopping when I'm preening in the camping gear display window at Flounder Pro Shops.

Chapter 6

When I was a teenager on a collision course with boy crazy, I gobbled up the amnesia cases, dream sequences, and partner swapping of *All My Children*. That's when I first saw her. She rivaled Sophia Loren for the most beautiful woman I had ever beheld, and I wanted to look just like her. Susan was a take-no-prisoners force of nature when I was singing Rubber Ducky with my five-year-old. Years later, armed with too many glasses of wine, a case of Girl Scout cookies, and only one American TV channel, I welcomed her into my living room in Spain. *Mi casa es su casa.*

Susan never aged, never had a bad hair day, and never got a pimple. An acquaintance once told me I looked like "that soap opera star." I could scarcely draw enough breath to ask, "Do you mean Susan Lucci?"

"No, that other one," she snorted. "I can't remember her name."

When otherwise literate people snort, it's time to take up llama herding in Peru. I have never forgotten the crushing sense of disappointment and humiliation.

I never cheated in school, so I didn't want to copy off Susan, but ten years later a pair of earrings she wore were still haunting me, so I figured the statute of limitations on copycat accessorizing had passed. It was longer than I had waited before adopting Linda Evans'

Dynasty hairstyle. My kids look at pictures of me from that time with absolute horror.

Daughter: "I can't believe we let you leave the house looking like that!"

Me: "It was all the rage in the eighties."

Daughter: "Mom, your bangs are sticking straight up. It looks like you're walking into the wind wherever you go."

Me: "Quit being so judgy!"

Daughter: (Miming walking into the wind.)

Pore me

I was a late bloomer, but when I finally developed breasts and lost the "baby fat," I had a knockout figure. I also had the unfortunate complexion that with make-up and a ski mask was barely noticeable. Luckily, when men talk to young women, their eyes are not trained on the lady's face. This focal preoccupation rendered any acne problem moot. I went straight from blemishes to wrinkles, but by that time, my breasts had drifted south and men's eyes had drifted north. Time to pull out the big guns.

Bear with me one moment while I set up a metaphor, which will likely be overused by the end of this book. One year, I had a vegetable garden and planted five zucchini seeds. They were so prolific that soon, the

Chapter 6

neighbors shut their blinds and locked their doors when they saw me coming from the garden with my wagon full of zucchini.

As the number of seniors increase, the anti-aging industry is zucchiniing at an alarming rate. At one time, baby boomers advocated going natural, burning their bras, and doing the streak. Now, they are attacking nature with an arsenal of anti-aging ammunition, and — thankfully — not doing the streak.

Of all the new wrinkles making their way onto my face, the most disturbing is the marionette mouth. You know the one: when the jowl lines running from your nose to your chin frame your mouth in a farcical puppet-like arrangement. It's especially creepy-looking if you sit in a guy's lap (make sure you know where his hands are at all times).

Many seniors have chosen to fight wrinkles by introducing toxins into their systems in the form of Botox. The *clostridium botulinum* bacteria responsible for botulism paralyzes the muscles in your skin, which would otherwise cause contractions, hence wrinkles. Since my bank account consists of small change and a ball of lint, I'm thinking injections of undercooked turkey gravy would work just as well.

Advertisers insist you can get the same results as Botox with any number of products on the market. Susan has her own line of beauty products, but since I had two checks bounce last month, I purchased a bargain "skin care system." Previously, my skin care routine had been washing with some "grainy stuff" from the grocery store and using hemorrhoid ointment under my eyes as needed for bags. I strongly recommend you keep a separate tube for your nether regions, and *don't mix up the tubes*!! Now, armed with my 30-day supply of a skin care system, better suited to a laboratory than a bathroom, I began my experiment. Please be assured no little baby bunnies or kittens were harmed in the testing of these products.

After several months of faithful use, I was still not seeing the startling results that were promised. Yes, the age spots have faded a little, but my complexion still leans closer to Ed McMahan than to Susan Lucci.

My family recommended I seek professional help, but the psychiatrist told me to get out of his office and find an esthetician. I went to a spa for a series of facial treatments. As soon as the relaxing massage began, the lights went out. I didn't know that narcoleptic comas are good for your skin.

I also had three sessions of microdermabrasion, with the promise of smaller pores, fewer age spots, and a glowing complexion. Despite compliments from friends and family, the only glow I could see was the lotion used to calm down the inflammation from having my face buffed with fine grit sandpaper.

Make-up your mind
The next logical step was camouflage. Until recently, I hadn't worn make-up in years. I still know how to lighten up the valleys and darken the hills to sculpt my fat nose and lack of cheekbones into works of art. I've even seen the dawn of airbrush make-up. This would be the way to go if I wanted to look like a mermaid on the side of a van. I want to know who looked into the mirror one morning and said, "You know what would make my face look better? Spray paint!"

I just never figured out how to find the right base color. Do you match the foundation to the light areas or the age spots? Do you coat your under-eyes in concealer before or after the foundation? Do you bother with foundation at all when you know damn well you're not going to put it on unless you're meeting the President of the United States?

We have lift-off
In my thirties, I had a long cylindrical skin tag on my upper eyelid that hung down far enough it got in my line of vision. There are two basic types of skin tags: lumps and noodles, and mine was definitely a noodle. You

don't generally see young people with skin tags; I always thought they were reserved for crones you see in fairytales. Since my first noodle appeared, I've lasered off multiple skin tags. When your face hangs down enough to block your vision, cosmetic skin care systems alone aren't going to cut it. Even spray paint won't take the place of surgical de-croning.

Many anti-aging creams, serums and lotions claim to be an alternative to a facelift, but sometimes there's just no substitute for the real thing. When you start to look like Marlon Brando in *The Godfather*, it's time for a jowl reduction. If you're sporting the latest in wattles, you may want to spring for a neck lift. There are plenty of over-the-counter products that can't replace cosmetic surgery, and very few facial flaws that cosmetic surgery can't replace.

I'm at the age where some days I open my eyes in the morning and see my eyelids. They resemble automatic garage doors in that the upper lids slide up under the puffy brow area, which droops enough to partially block my vision, and flops up and down when I do jumping jacks. You know it's time to take action when you sleep on your side and wake up to find your eyelids lying on the pillow.

Now that men's attention has shifted north on me, I'm considering blepharoplasty (eyelid surgery). Mostly,

Chapter 6

I'm considering how I can avoid it. The best way might be to invest in mastopexy (breast lift) so men's attention will once again move south.

I can watch many kinds of surgical procedures on TV without so much as flinching, but show me a plastic surgery procedure and I'm retching within seconds. There's something obscene about pulling the skin away from somebody's face. I'm too chicken to have people getting knives anywhere within the same zip code as my eyes, and I'd probably be the unfortunate patient whose ear accidentally falls off during the procedure.

I never could understand why people would want liposuction. While most surgeons are going small, using laparoscopic surgery for minimal invasiveness: plastic surgeons are invading to ridiculous extents. "Let's stick a vacuum cleaner hose under the skin and wave it around vigorously." After all the damage and bruising, you've removed a relatively small amount of fat. There have to be better ways to lose a couple pounds that don't include purging, enemas, or household appliances.

Hair Club for dignity
I come from a long line of women with thinning hair. My grandma had styrofoam heads on her dresser, magically sprouting hair like Chia Pets. I've heard it said that baldness in men is bad, but baldness in women is

devastating. That's totally unfair. Most men would rather glue a piece of road kill to their heads, try to rock a ridiculous looking comb-over, or wear a ball cap for the rest of their natural lives than admit that they're follicly challenged. Yul Brenner was one of a handful of white men who could make baldness look good. Even Sinéad O'Connor, in the women's camp, couldn't tempt me to rock the naked noodle look.

Minoxidil was pretty new when my hair started thinning on top. In a desperate attempt to slow down a hair strand Exodus to rival the Israelites' flight into the desert, I started squirting the stuff on my head every morning and before bed.

There's a funny thing about pillows. Sometimes the back of your head is on them, and other times the side of your face is smooshed in. The unfortunate effect of minoxidil on my pillowcase was that I started to sprout sideburns. It didn't take long to realize I cannot rock the Elvis look.

Die with a "t"

As I looked over the list of desirable foods for my new diet, it read like a who's who of edibles that cause emissions better blamed on the dog. I've taken to feeding Colt leftover beans to help validate my claims. On the

Chapter 6

plus side, I can eat all the parsnips I want. Unfortunately, I'm not even sure what a parsnip is.

My mission for week one was to take a before picture (ugh!), take my measurements, and track everything I put in my mouth. My foot gets extra points for humiliation. As I measured my breasts, my hands got clammy. I moved on to my waist and felt a chill running up my spine. By the time I got to my hips, I was getting too dizzy to read the numbers. Doggedly, I pushed on to my thigh. The tape measure was swallowed up. I think it's still in there somewhere.

Actually, I only need to lose twenty pounds to get to my target weight. *Only* 20 pounds! That's like three nervous little Chihuahuas. I guess I should be thankful I don't have to lose a golden retriever. I was told by my friend to dress "fat" when I went to my first weight loss meeting, so I wouldn't annoy people of a girth larger than mine. What does that mean? Should I stuff extra Chihuahuas in my shirt?

My first shopping trip after I started the diet, I had to take my points calculator into the store. It's a nice little gadget, but has the unfortunate appearance of a case for a diaphragm. If I buy a box of condoms, people will assume I'm going to get lucky, while they wonder why I'm poking at a diaphragm in the frozen foods aisle.

I was totally up for the challenge. I deeply admire all those people who are able to lose weight and keep it off. My vanity was at stake, my blood sugar was at stake, and my Chihuahuas just wanted to go home.

On the ball
You don't have to be creative to increase your visibility. I'm referring, again to gaining weight, which for most people is a fairly simple process. The ways to lose weight are complex, varied, and potentially hazardous to your health.

Since I'm not made of money, and find the smell of 60 other people's sweat slightly off-putting, I bought an exercise video. After only four weeks of feeling the burn, I could no longer stomach the same daily banter from my video trainer, so I opted instead for book learning. I started by fishing out a Yoga book I had used in high school. I quickly decided I was not up to "The Buttered Pretzel" position so I found a book of Yoga for seniors and decided to start out easy with "The Tree." How hard could it be to stand up straight and breathe at the same time? Let's just say I pray never to get pulled over for a field sobriety test.

Since balance was beyond me, the next logical choice was to sit on a ball. Somehow, this was going to firm my

Chapter 6

abdominals and give me buns of steel. What it gave me was bruises and rug burns.

As I was looking at the brightly colored still pictures in my instruction book, it failed to register that *balls roll*. I got pretty good at the "rolling backwards to a prone position on the floor from a sit" exercise. This should be accompanied with bulging eyes. Don't forget to inhale through the nose, and exhale profanities through the mouth. Follow this up with "sitting on an inflatable donut" exercise for the next 3 to 4 days.

What's purple and blue and spread all over?
Unfortunately, there is no punch-line. Remember the good old days when all you worried about on the beach was belly fat and cellulite? All that was required was an industrial strength lycra bathing suit with a little skirt.

WebMD has a slide show with information on varicose veins. I swear, one of the slides was, "What are the symptoms?" Unless you always wear slacks, everyone around you will be able to diagnose your condition. My method of diagnosis for almost anything is "poke at it," and even I can recognize varicose veins from across a crowded room. I don't need to get into poking range.

My first pregnancy, I developed them on my lady parts. One possible symptom is a dull aching sensation in the local area (anatomical – not geographical). It's a good thing I had a job on my feet, because sitting held all the attraction of feeding rabid wolverines in a petting zoo.

Now that pregnancy is a distant memory, my varicose veins have migrated to where they rightfully belong. There are two advantages of having them on my legs:

I can wear hideously ugly support hose;

As I get older, sitting is good.

Quasimodo

Once I started pre-menopause, my doctor wanted to run a bone density scan to get a baseline reading. To my surprise, I already had osteopaenia (light bone loss). When I returned to work after I got the test results, I immediately ran into the rest room to look for any telltale signs of a dowager's hump. I stood in profile, studying long and hard. If I'd had a pimple on my shoulder, I probably would have freaked out.

I have a friend who is absolutely beautiful, except she's got a hump. Are my eyes drawn to her perfect cheekbones, lovely complexion, great figure? No. I hate that I'm looking at her shoulder when I talk to her, but I can't look away. My family, who can never resist a chance to make me squirm, decided to tease me.

Me: "Does my right shoulder look bigger to you?"

Chapter 6

Daughter: "Don't worry; no one will ever notice it."
Me: (Panicky) "Notice what?"
Daughter: "They hardly look any different, really."
Me: "They? What are you trying to say?"
Son: "Don't worry, I think they have an opening to work at the bell tower of Notre Dame Cathedral."
Me: "I'm not that good with heights."

I was pretty sure they were joking, but I picked up a book on conversational French just in case.

Just a formality

I decided that before I lost my figure (done), I should get a really slinky formal gown. I used this gown for my second wedding, but it could easily have graced any red carpet runway. I decided my dress and I should go out someplace nice. I looked for a likely charity dinner, but choked at the price tag. Did my dress want to go out badly enough to rent a tux for my husband, park downtown and pay $500 a plate? My fuzzy bathrobe decided for me.

I can always count on my fuzzy robe to talk me out of ridiculous things like:
- Taking a walk in the rain
- Buying the perfect Christmas present for my husband on Black Friday
- Mowing the lawn

- Sitting in a football stadium in five degree temperature
- Participating in the annual lumberjack festival. (My log rolling skills are epic!)

My robe likes to curl up on the couch with a good book, while petting my dog and drinking hot cocoa. That's probably why I can no longer fit into my slinky formal gown. If you don't have a robe to blame for your poor life choices, I recommend you put down your hot cocoa and get one right away. It's a lot cheaper than a $500 per plate dinner.

That woman looks just like my mom
When was the first time you looked in the mirror and saw your mom or dad? I didn't mark it on my calendar in bold letters. I just hoped I would look like myself again when the hangover wore off. I know my mom is pretty, so I don't know why I felt shocked. Of course, I wouldn't dare to tell her that (she still has wooden spoons and a fairly good swing).

I don't curl up in a fetal position when I see her in the mirror anymore. My mom looks nothing like Susan Lucci, but I hope I look as good as Mom in twenty-two years—and I'm not even hung over.

Chapter 7
Financial Preparations for a Penniless Retirement

Eventually, we have to face the harsh reality that we should have started investing for retirement from the time we were waiting tables in high school. If you want to play the lottery, it's probably no more risky than 401(k) Roulette. Instead of whining about only having $50 and a coupon for seventy-five cents off when you buy three cases of Ramen noodles, you can laugh in the face of conventional fiscal wisdom. Is it too late to invest in beachfront property in Iceland? Will genealogical research yield us a long-lost rich uncle? If you can't find an inheritance, you may be forced to grow zucchini in your back yard. It grows like weeds and has to have some kind of nutritional value. Thank goodness for our safety net: the Social Security System. Whoever is laughing, cut it out!

What portfolio?

There are commercials for brokerage firms that will make your retirement dreams become a reality. There are also commercials for whole life insurance so that your family will have just enough money for a burial, which doesn't involve a broken down pickup truck, a cliff, and a gallon of lighter fluid. There seems to be a disconnect there. If I can be assured of a comfortable retirement, there should be enough money for a dance band and an ice sculpture at my wake. At the very least, I want a DJ and catering by Billy Bob's Barbecue. To get from point A. ($50 in my checking account) to point B. (comfortable and carefree golden years) requires last minute, panic-stricken financial planning.

My husband and I originally had a financial goal of drifting along aimlessly in a sea of indecision. Until recently, we were rocking that with dedication and eyes on the prize. There was no life-shattering event that spurred us to think seriously about the future, except that:

a. We aren't getting any younger
b. We aren't getting any richer.

Whenever some commercial would tell me to call my attorney or talk to my financial advisor, I would just roll my eyes. In the real world people have pizza delivery on speed dial, not a broker. But since I didn't want to spend

Chapter 7

my retirement working at Roscoe's Weiner Emporium on Main Street (try the slaw dogs), I figured some financial advice couldn't hurt.

"Jeff" made us a net worth statement and a cash flow summary. By the time he finished explaining the first pie chart, my eyes had glazed over. In order to retire by age 65, our first year retirement saving goal was $48,000 and a flock of goats. (Do goats come in flocks?) Call me delusional, but I actually thought that by changing to the bargain brand toilet paper, we could swing it. As a compromise, I quit my job to take up writing and goat herding. Did I just dream about goats as I slept through the meeting?

We've found we can scrape by on one income, as long as saving for the future reverts to wishful thinking. With market downturns pooping on our current retirement savings, the only thing at present between us and a future of dumpster diving is my writing skill. So far the rejection notices have been pretty kind, except for the agent who said, "Get a real job, loser." If my mom is the only person who buys a copy of this book, you can assume I'm a shopping cart wrangler at Uber-Mart.

Your chances are 1 in 100,000,000,000,000
Every Sunday on his way home from breakfast, my husband stops and buys one lottery ticket, which he

"powers up" to increase his potential retirement windfall. He reinvests his winnings of $9.00 to $12.00 each week, carefully weighing risk against return. My husband likens the waiting game to fishing. Out of a whole lake, will he drop his lure in front of a fish? Will the fish be interested and take the bait? Will he run the boat over a submerged log, tipping his wife into alligator infested waters? If his answer to any of the above is "no," it's too soon to cut bait.

I got a fortune cookie recently that said luck was on the way, so I immediately ran out and bought my own lottery ticket. What I failed to notice was the fortune cookie didn't specify what kind of luck. I wish I had noticed that before my brakes failed in the church parking lot. Next time Janet Mays and Evelyn Turner will know better than to swap cookie recipes on the front sidewalk after the service.

Bad luck is nothing new to me. Never get in line behind me at the supermarket, because the person in front of me will have a shoebox full of coupons, three items missing barcodes, and a bag of unidentifiable root vegetables.

I once went to a party where all the guests went down to the lake to fish. People ten feet to either side of me were pulling in blue gills the moment their lines hit the water. I didn't even get a nibble. I'd be lucky just to

Chapter 7

have a house with a view of that lake. I've often wondered, "Why couldn't I catch anything, and where did our host get all those fishing poles?" Honestly, I've spent less time worrying about global warming.

If it's Friday the 13th, I recommend you avoid playing the lottery, even if the mega jackpot is twenty-three million and some loose change found under the couch cushion. You stand a better chance of finding a herd of water buffalos drinking margaritas (no salt) in your laundry room.

Don't let my run of bad luck stop you from this popular method of saving for retirement. With my lottery ticket having no prayer of winning, your chances have just improved to 1 in 99,999,999,999,999.

401(k) Roulette
Like Paul Revere, economists have been sounding the alarm that Social Security benefits will be gone by the time we're ready to retire. They spout propaganda that our only hope for the future is to save for retirement in a 401(k) Plan or IRA. These are the sedans of retirement investment vehicles, against a passbook savings account, which is the subway. Of course, no bank outside of Bhutan uses passbooks any more.

In today's economy, even those seasoned professionals in the pension benefits industry are scratching their heads and stuffing their mattresses. Whereas the question used to be about balancing risk against return, or ROTH vs. tax deferred, we are now faced with a timing dilemma. The number of baby boomers barreling down on retirement is zucchiniing out of control, and they are all aiming for the same freeway off-ramp. I don't know how the ensuing traffic jam will affect the market, but I can just about guarantee all the rest stop ladies' rooms will be closed for cleaning.

In a blinding switch of metaphors, investing in stock means knowing when to get off the bus. I know I'm supposed to watch for bulls and bears in the market place, usually found somewhere near the produce section. *"Clean up on aisle six!"* If your 65th birthday falls on a day when the market is falling, you should develop a taste for tripe. During the most recent market downturn, my assets fell to half of their prior value: not a good time to have to cash in. It makes the subway look more and more attractive. Now I just have to move to Bhutan.

I had thought about buying stock in petroleum products, but a more realistic solution to the 401(k) dilemma is to roll my money over into a sure thing like peanut butter. The advantages are:
- Peanut butter tastes better than petroleum products

Chapter 7

- It's high in protein
- It's cheaper than meat
- It's a renewable resource
- It's versatile (see my peanut butter diet plan).

As retirees are forced to eat rice, beans, and peanut butter sandwiches I'll be rolling in dough.

Prune in the sun

As we get to the stewed prune for breakfast age, most of us develop less tolerance for the cold: my parents spent half of each year in Arizona, in the RV which now resides in my daughter's backyard, and may well be my retirement home. Many seniors are opting for retiring in a tropical paradise with a lower cost of living. You too can buy beachfront property for pennies on the dollar in Costa Rica ... 25 years ago.

Now you can choose from a lovely beachfront condominium for half a million dollars, or a parcel of undeveloped land in the jungle with plenty of streams for a guaranteed water source, going for the bargain price of a fully loaded Mercedes. When the ad says their highest priority is to get quality power, water and sewer into the community, you know you're getting in on the ground floor of a retirement dream.

When you add to this the expense of carting building materials for your villa by donkey to this remote mountaintop, your retirement dream could turn into a Tim Burton movie, complete with creepy animated characters and no butter on your popcorn. On the plus side, the views are insanely incredible; there's plenty of good rooting for your pig when you let him out in the morning; and you can enjoy the bracing 100% humidity on your two-hour hike to the nearest town.

If neither option appeals to you, (recapping: beachfront poverty or an outhouse in the jungle) make your escape from the high cost of living in the U.S., and check out the special expatriate deals in Venezuela.

That ship has sailed
Seattle is a relatively young city. The first settlers arrived there 100 years before I was born. Family legend has it that my great-great grandfather considered buying a little piece of real estate known as Mercer Island in Seattle. He decided he didn't want to row his boat to work every day, so he passed on it. It's hard now to find a single-family home on Mercer Island for less than a million dollars. Real estate heiress is not on my résumé.

There are any number of lucrative investment opportunities which never even crossed my mind back in the day. It seems rather pointless now to:
- Sell pet rocks
- Start a folk song and ballad singing career

Chapter 7

- Become a Tupperware lady
- Buy stock in Atari, Beta, and 8 tracks
- Design a line of gaucho pants and bolero jackets
- Invent the electric percolator, or
- Invest in spray starch.

When I was growing up, my parents had a "bubble car". It was an Isetta, made by BMW back in the 50s. The only door on it was the whole front of the car. It swung open, steering wheel and all. I often wonder if it would be worth something now. It would be just my luck if my folks had kept it, and my inheritance was moldy smelling, and impossible to get parts for.

Lower your standards

Most of us can live more simply than we are at present. Start with things you can live without: beer, porn, smoking, off-track betting, and crack cocaine. Then examine the places you can cut back, like avoiding spending on a manicure by having your nails chewed off by wolverines.

Currently, I buy a hideously expensive brand of dog food for optimum nutrition. If Colt's nutritional requirements are not met, he supplements his diet by eating poop. We might have to put up with cheaper dog food and bad breath. I definitely will not be encouraging mouth kisses from my puppy.

If your mortgage is getting on top of you, I have two words: mobile home. Who wouldn't want to see their neighbors on cop shows? You can dress up your dream home with fake grass on your plywood porch, and a bench car seat in front. An awning and picnic table are nice touches, but not required. Check the neighborhood covenants to see if you're allowed to take your lights down after Christmas.

Drop in the saddle
There are those who wouldn't know what to do with themselves if they didn't have a job. They are happiest when running a business eight-plus hours each day, and golfing on the weekends well past sixty-five. They are generally type A people, who already have a comfortable nest egg for retirement. We hate them all.

Now there is an increasing number of people who must go into indentured service beyond 65 in order to pay the bills. I have friends who are in the trenches 40 hours a week to get supplemental health insurance through work, to cover what Medicare won't pay. Others work part time so they don't have to *live* in trenches.

This is obviously the least desirable retirement plan option. Statistical reports predict there will be a growing number of disgruntled seventy year-olds in the work place over the next twenty years. I hope these are not the

Chapter 7

same people who started collecting firearms as a hobby for their mid-life crisis.

Many people choose to seek inventive ways to work all their lives, without it feeling like work. You might wish to avoid joining the circus, professional bull riding, working on a coffee boat, or field-testing parachutes. In short, leave the flagpole painting to someone who won't snap a hip in a strong wind.

The last Girl Scouts
Every time I see a commercial showing people who have managed to beat the system, I want to shake my TV. Where does this person get off bragging about reducing what he owes the IRS by $150,000? And how the heck do you end up owing more to the IRS than I earned in three years (when I had a real job)? Has debt really become a game of hot potato? Is the point to pass along your tax obligation to everyone else? Little wonder the government can't save the social security system.

For generations the accepted cure for widespread economic hysteria was to find somebody to blame. The problem in the current economy is that there are just too many likely candidates for the job of scapegoat. How about this time around we pin it on the lawyers who work for the IRS? If they can't shake down Mr. TV commercial for the $150,000 he owes, I think we can agree the IRS has it coming.

As young people, our generation tried to make the world a better place, even if we went about it in pretty stupid ways at times. If I'm proud of my generation for only one thing it is this:
- 6 out of 10 people aged 51 to 61 in the U.S. fear they won't have enough money to retire on
- As many as 32% of boomers face a penniless retirement
- Most of us seek reasons and solutions more enthusiastically than we seek somebody to blame
- Conventional wisdom doesn't allow the use of bullets to explain "one thing." You can blame it on my editor for letting it slide.

Chapter 8
Ordering off the Senior Menu

What's left after I remove fat, carbs, and salt from my diet? Cardboard. Somehow, aging also requires you eat your dinner of cellulose at 4:00 PM. While you're digesting, you can take your biochemical degree and develop a diet rich in anti-oxidants and polyphenols to fight the free radicals carpet-bombing your body every day. We do this so *The Today Show* doesn't mistakenly announce our 100th birthday on TV.

The senior smorgasbord
For years I looked longingly at the senior menu with its great prices and smaller portions. I don't need two pounds of grits with my Golden Glutton breakfast, and I don't want to pay extra for grits I won't eat,[13] so why can't they make a senior menu for pre-seniors? After dyeing my gray roots, spending a fortune on anti-wrinkle

---

[13] Three-fourths of Americans and most of the known world would put <u>all</u> grits into this category.

cream, and dressing in junior department shirts that leave no doubt whether I'm an inny or an outy, there's something intrinsically self-defeating about trying to pass myself off as older than I am, just to save a few bucks. I'd even be willing to stop swiping jelly packets if they'd let me legitimately order just half a Reuben sandwich at a discount price.

Is there some unwritten rule about senior pricing only being offered earlier in the day? Normally, my husband and I sleep in on the weekends and have breakfast in our favorite 24-hour diner at 3:00 – 4:00 p.m. (Oh, like you've never slept for fourteen hours on a Saturday night.) This left us competing for seating with the retired dinner crowd. These days I secretly look longingly at their chicken fried steak as I chew my bacon. Sure I have grease, but they have (sigh) gravy.

Will I ever have a special day set aside to skip church and ignore the laundry when I retire? Am I doomed to spend every day of the week during my golden years eating dinner at 4:00 and being in my jammies by 8:00? For now, I think I can safely say that if you see me at the diner eating dinner at 4:00, it's only because I skipped the bacon in favor of gravy.

Indigestion on rye

Chapter 8

Do you know why you don't see senior menus at most Mexican restaurants? It's because seniors don't have any business eating refried beans! The introduction of enchiladas to the senior gastro-intestinal system is an all-out assault on weakening sphincters. This can cause reflux and heartburn; and it gives me a good excuse to use the word *sphincter* in a sentence.

If you have noticed signs of impaired gastric motility, never fear! Irregularity spokesperson, Jamie Lee Curtis, explains with secret hand signals and vague charts that yogurt can help you poop. This is good, because inability to pay for new crowns on every molar will make it impossible to gum your high fiber cereal.

Apricot couscous, mango chutney, avocado-grapefruit relish: what do all these dishes have in common? They are desperate attempts to camouflage recipes for digestive health. I have personally never eaten an eggplant, stuffed filo dough, or curried anything. I stay away from recipes that include jicama, shiitake mushrooms, capers, anchovies, or parsnips. If I had the resources to afford more than box macaroni and cheese, I still wouldn't eat fresh artichokes.

Even those recipe books that tout fast, easy, "homey" food end up with ingredients that sound like they belong in the credits of a foreign film, and vegetables cut into matchsticks. Let's get real, people. Yes, we want meals that won't pass through us like the bullet train, but lentils will always be a hard sell at the dinner table.

I won't sugarcoat it: prunes make you poop. As you get older, pooping is good. Unfortunately, the sulfur used in the drying process can cause derriere emissions that will clear a room faster than a bomb scare. Between poop and gas, prunes had to clean up their image. Many manufacturers are now selling "dried plums". They're not fooling anybody. We all know that dried plums are what your grandmother stewed for breakfast to get grandpa out of her hair for a few hours.

It's time for an honest diet plan with a name like "Better Bland Food." Admit that "pâté" is a four-letter word. I know it's disgusting but it's good for you, so stop whining and eat your goose liver. I'm just waiting for a cookbook that says, "Despite your best efforts, this will take two weeks to prepare and will only taste mildly interesting."

Who emancipated the radicals?

While Ponce de Leon tramped through Florida swamps looking for the fountain of youth, modern man tramps through the bookstore. Not only do you avoid bloodsucking gators, mosquitos, and leeches, but your quarry will be categorized by subject and shelved alphabetically by author. It beats looking for a fountain in

Chapter 8

a swamp. Diet books urge you to battle the free radicals in your system with antioxidants and polyphenols. Free radicals are created by ultraviolet rays, smoking, air pollution and (guess what) normal aging. They contribute to heart disease, cancer, and inflammatory conditions.

I have no trouble recognizing vitamins C and E to start my antioxidant campaign, but I have to wonder if Coenzyme Q10 is a figment of somebody's overactive imagination. I once owned a Mazda 626, but I bet they would have sold more cars if they'd given the model a sexier name, like the Mazda Lynx. Even a Mazda Woodchuck would have been more interesting. Likewise, antioxidants should have names that mean something to real people.

Since lipoic acid is the antioxidant equivalent of non-chlorine bleach, it should be called "Vita-Boost". Besides increasing production and absorption of other antioxidants, it is a cure for "incurable" mushroom poisoning. "Shroom Toxin Terminator" might be a good name if it didn't take so long to say and didn't sound like a super hero. Stan Lee would have a field day creating a fungal crime fighter.

What foods contain antioxidants? Look for key words such as "fresh," "whole," "complex," "unrefined", and "low fat". These can be found in supermarkets where customers have their personal shoppers load cloth bags of groceries into their Mercedes-Benzes while they sip coffee at the Starbucks next door. These foods are a little harder to find in stores that offer double coupon specials on Wednesdays.

Alternatively, you can join the emaciated pale crowd at health food stores and buy packets of daily supplements. One plan I've read required 13 vitamins and supplements a day, to go with your seven to ten servings of fruits and vegetables. For just tens of dollars a day, you can take handfuls of pills to reduce your medical risks, by heading off every free radical known to modern science. If you want a slower more ineffective way to enjoy your supplements, try rubbing vitamin C all over your body.

Did I mention in the indigestion section that many people suffer from heartburn, from taking too many pills?

No salt, no fat, no taste

Short-term memory loss is one of the first indications of impaired brain function due to aging. Recent studies have linked belly fat in your 40s to a higher rate of dementia as early as your 60s. My grandmother lived to be 92, and was sharp as a tack to the end. My great grandmother spent her final years in restraints,

Chapter 8

screaming non-stop. The difference: before great-grandma shrank down to skin and bones, she did her clothes shopping in the "husky" section of the dry goods store. On the other hand, my grandmother was always average size. Since my anecdotal evidence totally supports the scientific findings, I think we can agree that overweight Americans are mentally doomed.

Since the introduction of margarine in 1910, the death rate from heart attack in the U.S. has increased from 3,000 in 1930 to half a million in 1960. Since free radicals are also swimming in trans-fat (they prefer the breaststroke), anti-aging experts agree that if you eat chocolate éclairs or cheesecake and survive to old age, your heart may be beating the odds, but the free radicals will leave you looking like a mummy on a good day.[14]

At a relatively early age, my blood pressure started going up. I had followed in my mother's footsteps when cooking, which necessitated buying a salt mine to make one meatloaf. Since salt was destined to melt my neurons down faster than Chernobyl, I faced the choice between flavor and both halves of my brain functioning. My family is already questioning my brain function, so I can't afford to lose any more gray matter. It would be pretty embarrassing to have a stroke and nobody noticed a difference.

---

[14] January 18, 1042 B.C., just after dinner

Going from a high salt diet to a low salt diet was quite a shock to my taste buds. I decided it was definitely a good time for some self-pity. Low fat dieters can buy fat-free foods with increased salt content, which masquerade as real food. Low sodium dieters have a choice of bland or blander. Most prepared foods are high in salt, so forget about my specialty: boxed macaroni and cheese.

For those who have both high blood pressure and high cholesterol, prepare for a diet of plain oatmeal and styrofoam packing peanuts. You'll live longer, but why would you want to?

Just desserts

About one in one hundred children will develop Type 1 (Juvenile) Diabetes. One in ten people will develop Type 2 (Adult Onset) Diabetes, usually due to diets rich in cream puffs and bacon. As obesity becomes more widespread (pun intended), the incidence of Type 2 is increasing.

For years I claimed I was watching my weight because diabetes runs in the family. What a load of hooey! I'm watching my weight because vanity also runs in my family. I'm genetically doomed to freak out if I get a wart, let alone a gut.

Chapter 8

Unfortunately, I've inherited my dad's sweet tooth. Go to any potluck and Dad would head straight for the dessert table. I like anything fruity, gummy, or chewy, so long as it has a glycemic index of at least "holy cow!!!" Two months ago my metabolism hit a brick wall. I can almost tell you to the day when it shut down. It has taken me two months to gain ten pounds; it should take me two years to lose it. That's assuming I diet and exercise daily. Phbbt![15]

After raising kids, I always associated sugar with extra energy. Then I went to a workshop where we were given a cup of sugar and a weight. After lifting the weight with the right hand, we held the sugar in the left and lifted the weight again. The weight was supposed to feel heavier because the body feels weaker when exposed, even indirectly to sugar. I frequently think of that illustration as I'm hefting a one-pound bag of M&Ms. Sure enough, that puppy can feel pretty heavy if I'm holding a bottle of Yoo-Hoo[16] in the other hand.

I'm trying to reduce my sugar and carbohydrate intake to help head off any future blood sugar problems, but carbs include bread. I'd rather go skiing naked than give up bread. So if the supermarket is sold out of every loaf of bread, bagels, English muffins and rolls, I'll be

---

[15] Literal translation is, "time to buy larger jeans".

[16] Chocolate milk with a silly name

forced to eat my carbs in the form of fudge brownies—the staff of life. All you skiers can thank me now.

Danger, caramels ahead
I could eat a bag of candy orange slices in one sitting, and regret it for one week—repeat, ad infinitum. That was before my teeth had a falling out with my face. Since I love caramels, taffy and gummy orange slices, I've learned to chew very carefully. It's a dangerous game of, "Which tooth will be sucked out of my skull if I eat this?"

I have friends with dentures and partials, who face a much greater dilemma when presented with jellybeans than I do. Every day they play a game of dignity Russian Roulette. The loser gets to pick his teeth out of his neighbor's soup bowl.

"If I eat the gummy bears, will my teeth fall out onto the movie theater floor? If so, do I want them back?"

Besides the obvious, I have good cause to want to keep my teeth where they are. Whenever we visited my grandparents, grandpa Matti would serenade us during meals. Matti's dentures would move at a different speed from the rest of his mouth, creating a rather disturbing drum solo. I only have to chew too loudly to feel totally self-conscious. If I start clicking, I may as well sit at the same table as Lynn Newbottom. Lynn has an unfortunate belching problem, but if I time it right, her burps will drown out my dentures.

Tea for two

It's not enough to take away my salt, fats, and sugar; now you want to take away my caffeine? At some point, a person has to draw the line!

When I was a kid, I couldn't wait to drink coffee like grown-ups. The Finns were not satisfied with seeing who could bake the longest in the sauna. They also raced to see who could drink a cup of scalding coffee first. Coffee is not native to Scandinavia, but the Finns embraced it as yet another way to hurt themselves.[17]

When well meaning friends want to show me the error of my ways, sometimes snarky comments just pop unbidden out of my mouth.

"Would you like some herbal tea?" Karen asked. "I have some very nice chamomile."

"Do you have some very nice coffee?" I asked.

"I don't even keep it in the house! Caffeine is addictive and may lead to bone loss. I hear it can even cause miscarriages."

"Karen, I'm smack in the middle of menopause. I don't think a double espresso will decrease world

---

[17] Finland has the highest suicide rate of any country in the world. They just like to do it the hard way.

population," I argued. "And that would make my boss a drug dealer. We don't have herbal tea in the office because we're all addicted to staying awake during staff meetings. Besides that," I continued, "a study in France suggests caffeine can slow the decline of cognitive abilities in women. That would have been good to know last year when you got lost in the mall."

"I hate you," she snorted.

"Whoa! Time to switch to decaf."

Peanut butter diet

As a solution to getting antioxidants that won't break the bank, may I suggest trying my Peanut Butter Diet Plan.

You can get all the healthy legume-y goodness of peanuts with simple, innovative recipes. May I recommend the Cream of Peanut Soup, or the Moroccan Peanut Couscous? Whatever your budget, there is a peanut butter plate to please the fussiest palate.

Peanut butter in your diet will increase Omega-3 fatty acids, which contribute to heart health. Peanuts are low on the glycemic index, so provide proteins and complex carbohydrates that won't raise your blood sugar levels as high as most other carbohydrates.

What peanut butter won't do is:
- Prevent cancer
- Improve memory

Chapter 8

- Cure scurvy
- Reduce fine lines and wrinkles
- Counteract mushroom poisoning.

Feel free to try any of these recipes, which I got off the internet but was too indifferent to sample.

Citrus Peanut Sauce
  ½ cup creamy peanut butter
  ½ cup orange juice
  ½ cup lemon juice
  ½ cup soy sauce
  1 tablespoon sugar

Whisk until well blended. Use as a salad dressing or over pasta. If you're a thrill seeker, try it on ice cream.

Spinach with Peanut Sauce (Shut up — it's good for you)
  2 tablespoons vegetable oil
  3 onions, thinly sliced
  1 medium red bell pepper, seeded and chopped
  1½ cups vegetable stock
  ½ cup peanut butter
  2 tablespoons cider vinegar
  Cayenne pepper to taste
  As much spinach as you can force down, washed, de-stemmed and chopped.

Sauté onions and bell pepper in vegetable oil. Add the stock and bring to a boil. Add peanut butter and vinegar. Add small amounts of cayenne pepper to the sauce and taste. DO NOT taste the cayenne pepper before adding to sauce. Pour over stewed spinach. Serve or throw away immediately.

Peanut Soup
   1 stalk celery chopped
   ½ an onion chopped
   2 tablespoons heart healthy margarine
   1½ tablespoons flour
   4 cups chicken broth
   1 cup peanut butter (smooth or chunky)
   1 cup milk

Sauté celery and onion in margarine until onion is tender. Thoroughly blend in flour. Add chicken broth. Stir and cook until boiling and thickened. Remove from heat and strain. Blend in peanut butter and milk. Heat through but do not boil. Serve hot, cold, or blindfolded.

As long as you include vitamin C, vitamin E, bioflavenoids, lipoic acid, selenium, ginkgo biloba, aerobic exercise, weight training, Co Q10, and doctor-directed hormone therapy with your basic peanut butter diet, you can look forward to a long and healthy life.

Chapter 8

Holiday traditions

As seniors, we owe it to our children to pass along the meals that personalize and define our holidays.

Thanksgiving:

You'll need enough food to bring a solid oak table to its knees. A 25-pound turkey is a good place to start. Personally, I would not want to meet a 25-pound turkey in the wild. That puppy could run down your average Hybrid and scratch the hell out of your paint job.

Green bean casserole is becoming an increasingly popular side dish, while sweet potatoes should only be served if baked and garnished with a full bag of marshmallows on top. (Remove plastic bag before cooking). Be sure to include mashed potatoes and gravy, cranberry sauce, stuffing, and antacids with your meal.

Following a three-hour digestion break, serve any pumpkin pie the dog has not already eaten off the counter. Be sure to give thanks today, because you will spend the rest of the long weekend regretting your personal life choices … and eating leftovers.

Christmas:

This season is loaded with labor intensive, high fat goodies, which you can give as a gift to your disgustingly skinny cousin. I take homemade gingerbread boys to work, spreading office holiday cheer. Unfortunately, my son-in-law enjoys helping decorate. I seem to find a lot of cookies engaged in inappropriate behavior, or which have a hangman's noose around their doughy little necks.

We do not subject our family and friends to death by fruitcake. I don't think I could lift a fruitcake high enough to bludgeon them in any case. While visions of sugarplums are dancing in your head, I'll still be eating leftovers from Thanksgiving.

Girl Scout Cookie Time:
This little-recognized holiday is responsible for more regrets than all others combined. I was a Brownie leader during the great Girl Scout Cookie Campaign of '92. I gained a freezer stuffed with Trefoil shortbread cookies and twenty-five pounds stuffed in my pants during this ill-fated holiday season. Since few people request the shortbread cookies, I felt it my duty to buy and eat all leftover cases.

Since then, I am one of the few people who marches up to the table outside the supermarket and demands Trefoil Cookies. The girl scout leaders look at me with adoration and gratitude.

Halloween:

Chapter 8

As I write this, I'm scarfing down leftover Halloween candy. Need I say more?

As long as we have traditions, we have magic. I can't perform card tricks, but I can serve up clam chowder and flat bread on Christmas Eve, and my family acts as if I just pulled an elephant out of my hat. Eat that, David Copperfield.

Chapter 9
Where did I leave my memories?

Thank goodness we have photos and knick-knacks to remind us of rich defining moments in our lives. I have salmon steaks in the freezer from a fishing trip six years ago. Now I can't look at freezer burn without thinking of that day. There's no hiding the times I've lost my train of thought, but at least when I stop in my tracks with eyes glazing over, I can't see the pitying expressions of those around me. Believe me, you don't want to be arrested for vagrancy outside Starbucks, when trying to remember the difference between a tall and a grande. Usually bail is set at the price of a tall. I try to talk to friends my own age as much as possible, hoping they will have forgotten I have already told a particular story. I have no such luck with my kids, but at least they have the good grace to ignore me.

Chapter 9

Grandma's belly button

Everybody has one: a defining moment which forever scars a person. Once, a shameful piece of dirty laundry, these moments are now paraded on Jerry Springer as "delightful" eccentricities. For some, this is a single circumstance, but for others it is repeated serial humiliation.

My roots are in a small Finnish community. My forefathers emigrated from Finland to take advantage of logging, salmon fishing, and reindeer herding opportunities in Washington State. Undeterred by the lack of reindeer in the region, they looked for other ways to party on the weekends.

Little known fact: the Finns invented the sauna, which they also refer to as "bathhouse." Sauna was a weekly affair. Families would gather at the home of a neighbor who had a bathhouse for a night of communal bathing, and coffee-swilling debauchery. As the evening continued, the heat in the sauna increased, so the general order for bathing was:

- Girls
- Boys
- Women
- Men.

By the way, did I mention there was nudity involved?

For some reason, the boys never required an adult chaperone. This explains how they managed to bring the garden hose into the sauna once, to create more steam — effectively extinguishing the fire in the wood stove.

The girls always had Grandma riding shotgun. Regularly seeing your grandmother naked is, in itself, something most people can't claim. But it gets worse. Sometime during the course of the ordeal, my grandma always slung her soapy washrag over her finger and proceeded to dig her way to China via her belly button. Like a train wreck, you couldn't look away.

When I got married, I decided I needed a special rite of passage into womanhood. Most women would consider getting married and leaving home enough of a ritual, but not me. I had my sights set on washing my belly button without being told. This wasn't going to be the half-baked job I did under Grandma's tutelage, this would be the real thing. OK, it's not like the Finnish ritual was as severe as, say, tattooing a Maori warrior, but it took three days for the redness to fade away. My belly button lint will just have to stay where it is from now on.

The average shelf life of a thought
Short-term memory at our age can be as fleeting as a streaker in the Arctic. Why is it I can remember the theme

Chapter 9

song to Gilligan's Island, but can't remember what I ate for breakfast—literally? My standard answer to any pop quiz is Bismarck, North Dakota. Clearly, there are a few questions where that doesn't apply. You may ask, "Why would anyone care what you had for breakfast?" Obviously, they want to feel smug knowing they can remember their raisin bran, toast and coffee. I will just laugh when you report your car stolen from the spot fifteen spaces down from where you are actually parked.

Last night I dreamed I couldn't remember the word "to". In every sentence involving this slippery little preposition, my words would come to a grinding halt. You may have to backtrack over your day to find your car keys, but I had to search my lexicon for directional stunt doubles. Dreams are supposed to be your subconscious mind at work. I'm not sure whether or not I dream in color. Is the show over when you start dreaming in senile?

Thank goodness we spend our lives collecting souvenirs, mementos and photographs. I moved away from Homestead, Florida shortly before Hurricane Andrew hit in 1992. Friends who had evacuated returned and were unable to find their homes. There were no longer any street signs, familiar landmarks, or drug smuggling warehouses. Block after block was piled with tangled, broken trees. Most of my life's landmarks reside on the shelves of my living room bookcase. There are souvenirs of my trip to London, pottery from Spain, photos from countless vacations and Christmases. God forbid someone should break in and steal my knick-knacks. I would stumble around like an amnesia victim in a snowstorm. This is why the senior center offers scrapbooking the first Monday of every month. Bring your own hot glue gun.

When Samson forgot he was dating the enemy and got roaring drunk, he fell asleep and Delilah cut his hair (it would make a great clip on YouTube). His strength left him and he became the laughingstock of the Philistines. When I forgot weight and strength differences while walking three dogs, I broke my shoulder (also a winner for YouTube). I was the laughingstock of the emergency room. The stabbing victim next door actually felt sorry for me as I sat in my cubicle of shame.

Forgetfulness is my Kryptonite. I can be the family hero: bringing home a steady paycheck, cooking delicious dinners each night, giving the dog his arthritis medicine; but forget one little trip to the bank, resulting in several bounced checks, and nobody cares if I can outrun a speeding bullet. I think Stan Lee needs to create a new superhero with the power to remember the dry cleaning on Thursday nights.

Chapter 9

Since my memory is surprisingly good for really painful events, I feel compelled to share the angst with innocent bystanders. I had natural childbirth for both of my daughters—no drugs, no alcohol, no firearms. I would relate every painful second of labor and delivery to women in their last trimester of pregnancy, when it was too soon to blow and push but too late to use a condom.

Selective photographic memory
My kids are fully grown, but they want super powers. They will create their Superhero persona and come up with improbable scenarios, in which they will save the day. My youngest daughter's super power is to make people uncomfortable. Customer Service Representatives give her what she wants just to get her to leave.

I have a super power as well. I have a near-photographic memory for the tunes to TV theme songs and advertising jingles. I can't necessarily remember the words, but I can hum the heck out of them. Anyone can sing the themes from *Rawhide, Bonanza,* or *Mr. Ed.* Want to hear the tunes for *The Avengers, I Spy, The Rifleman,* or *My Favorite Martian*? I'm your gal!

"What possible good can come from this super power?" you may ask.

Imagine if some evil genius bent upon world domination takes over every television in the world. She controls the major networks and cable, pumping subliminal messages into broadcasts of reality shows. She promotes her agenda of euthanasia for everyone over 65, in order to save in healthcare costs and reduce the David Hasselhoff fan base.

I hum my little theme songs, which breaks the hold of the brainwash broadcast for those around me. I hum to the network programmers, breaking the spell for them. Every channel goes into syndication overload, and the world is safe from reality shows. Retirement age seniors breathe a collective sigh of relief, and get to watch Knight Rider marathons.

It could happen. I would be proud to hum for truth, justice, and the American way! (Cue Superman TV show theme song.)

Back in my day ...
Go to any restaurant gift shop and you can find pamphlets that give you the trends, favorite songs, and average price for a house in the year you were born. This has the unfortunate effect of making you think back to all the changes since you were a kid and realizing your lifetime has become "history." It also makes you wonder why a restaurant needs a gift shop.

Chapter 9

Highlights of the new old farts (some lying is involved):

1946 The Baby Boomer Generation begins, and the first bikinis go on sale in Paris. Cottage cheese thighs come out of the closet.

1947 UFO allegedly found in Roswell, NM. The U.S. begins mass production of weather balloons.

1948 First NASCAR race for modified stock cars is held at Daytona Beach. The term "redneck" is first coined by Jeff Foxworthy, Sr.

1949 First Polaroid land camera sold. Photographer complained, "You blinked" 60 seconds later.

1950 First television remote control is marketed. Joey Roenscheck becomes the first U.S. couch potato.

1951 First oral contraceptive (The Pill) is invented. The Pope pretends not to notice.

1952 Elizabeth II becomes Queen of England after the death of her father, George VI. Welsh Corgis invade Buckingham Palace.

1953 Playboy Magazine's first issue featured Marilyn Monroe. Magazines could be found under the mattresses of teenage boys within thirty-two minutes and sixteen seconds.

1954 President Dwight D. Eisenhower signs social security bill into law. Social Security system faces 1.2 million dollar deficit for the first time.

1955 Disneyland opens in California. The Magic Kingdom is rocked by scandal as Donald Duck is caught in public without pants.

1956 Elvis Presley releases his first hit: Heartbreak Hotel. First Elvis Presley impersonator hits Vegas strip.

1957 Peak of the Baby Boomer years, and foot-and-mouth disease reaches epic proportions in England. George Walker Bush was not to blame.

The closest we got to texting when I was a kid was prefixes like Trinity (TR), Sunset (SU), or Cherry (CH) on the phone numbers. Can you imagine the frustration of a teenager faced with a rotary dial phone? My daughter was eight years old when the Navy moved us to Spain, where the phone systems were a little behind the times. The first time she tried to use our home phone, she was confused as to why nothing happened when she punched the numbers in the little circles. I can just imagine someone trying to text on a rotary dial phone. That would make a great clip on YouTube!

Chapter 9

Our generation saw the dawn of the personal computer. In 1956, the first hard disk was born—it was five megabytes and had an optional ice maker. By the time I was in junior high school, I was part of an elite group who learned to operate a Hewlitt Packard the size of a mini-van. We had to learn binary and I punched the heck out of about twenty-five cards just to get a simple "loop" (that is, add two to the previous number, ad infinitum). I was obviously on the cutting edge of computer programming while cutting math class to punch chads out of my pre-DOS "floppy disks." I was now qualified to either go to college at MIT or vote in Florida.

In 1981, the first personal computer using DOS exploded onto the scene. I was so excited when we got our very own Commodore, and the first Dummies book was born. When the flashing cursor came up for the first time my palms started to sweat. I would have been more comfortable diving into an alligator-infested swimming pool than take a chance on typing in a command that might cause the computer to spit out profanities. It would be my luck to get a computer programmed by somebody with Tourette Syndrome.

In my lifetime, we've gone from typewriters and carbon paper to word processing, to texting: from triplicate to instant written communication. You could make a good argument that the evolution of communication is the single most important development in our lifetime. I would like to make a case for Post-it notes, first launched in 1981. It's somewhat more primitive than a computer notebook, but absolutely essential to those of us with no appreciable short-term memory … and they are available at restaurant gift shops.

Remember when:
- Celsius was centigrade?
- Ointment was salve?
- Lamb-chops was a puppet?
- The Beatles were fab?
- The blue plate was meat loaf?
- Seat belts were few?
- Bubble gum had baseball cards?
- TV was new?

Obviously. Emily Dickinson has nothing to worry about, and she probably never used bullets for her sonnets.

Ghosts of pets past
Part of the human condition is to form emotional attachments, which can last as memories all our lives, or until we forget our right from our left. We are fascinated

Chapter 9

by the animal kingdom and are quick to seek a connection with nature. Grizzly Adams had the right general idea, until he forgot where he put his fingers one day. Most people prefer dogs and cats to pets that can disembowel them.

There's a different breed of dog or cat to suit most any personality. Once an attachment is formed, the loss of a beloved pet can be devastating. It would be a great blow to Paris Hilton's wardrobe if she lost little Fluffy.

When I was in fourth grade, our family dog died. I was given the opportunity to choose our next dog. We wanted to exercise our right to bear arms, so bird-hunting seemed like a good family hobby and bonding experience. Once I learned to fire a shotgun, I chose a black Labrador retriever named Killer.

Killer showed all the enthusiasm for pheasant scent that I felt for skunk cabbage. She did, however, love to swim. She was not particular as to whether it was a lake, stream, mud puddle, or wet cow pie. One of the most powerful triggers for memory is the sense of smell, and I got to sit at ground zero of an olfactory event to rival Hiroshima in the back of the family station wagon.

Contrary to her cowardly nature, she saved me from an attack when she was old and crippled. I won't go into detail on this touching chicken soup moment, but she was willing to do anything and give everything to protect me. All the money in the world can't buy that kind of love; and it's something I will never forget.

Today, people are more understanding than they used to be if you need to shed a tear or two for a lost four-legged friend. Oddly, folks are not very understanding about arming your children or having manure smell in the back of the car.

Droning on

Of course, there's no point in childhood memories if you can't mercilessly share them with loved ones, acquaintances, and the creepy guy at the bus stop.

In my day, dinner usually consisted of potato soup, oatmeal, or fried dirt—and we were glad to have it. Mom was a housewife who provided a loving home, free of spiders and rabid skunks. Dad was home on weekends, wrestling with the kids, working jigsaw puzzles, and going on ill-fated fishing trips. My grandma regularly knitted me sweaters and ugly hats with tassels and earflaps on them.

I guess it's a natural part of the aging cycle to want to escape back to childhood. That's probably why I rhapsodize about the days of climbing trees, catching tadpoles, and getting my sneakers wet in rain-soaked fields. I *don't* fondly remember stacking firewood, ironing, pulling weeds from the vegetable garden, or

Chapter 9

ripping down derelict barns for the scrap lumber.[18] Perhaps my most traumatic experience growing up was when an earwig snuck into my pants on the clothesline, causing the worst strip-tease routine in the history of the Pacific Highway Texaco station.

I never realized how fearful American parents have grown until I moved out of the country. In Spain, life was older and simpler. If I lost track of my kids on the city streets, I would have no concern for their safety. I knew that complete strangers would care well for them and would make every effort, in spite of the language barrier, to reunite them with their family. The kids would probably get ice cream and mud dolls along the way. It gave my kids a chance to experience the kind of security I felt as a child. I wonder if we're the last generation to grow up in the "good old days?"

Repeating myself ... Repeating myself

If you hang out with me long enough, you will hear the same old story over and over. Sometimes, I'll have a vague sense of déjà vu as I'm relating the tale, but more often than not, it seems like a masterpiece of innovation. I count on friends my own age not to remember my average bowling score or how long I breastfed my kids.

---

[18] Parents: make sure your child's tetanus shots are up to date before callously exposing them to rusty nails.

My kids, however, remember each time I spin the same yarn, and are quick to point it out. If they had any manners, they would ignore what I'm saying. I've done it many times for them.

Then there's the problem of repeating words or phrases. I can't think of anyone else in the family with this strange condition, except my grandmother could never say "oy" less than three times in succession. Either sentence stuttering is not hereditary, or my family members are doing it when I'm not paying attention to what they're saying — again, a fairly common occurrence.

I have many good reasons for this phenomenon that don't include senility, and a couple that do. When my needle gets stuck, I figure the person didn't hear me the first time, since they didn't react with gales of laughter to my witty remark. I may also repeat something several times if I'm talking while someone else has the floor. It might seem rude, but I think seniors should have priority in Robert's Rules of Order. Miss Manners does not have jurisdiction over Parliamentary procedure.

My friend: "I think we should …"

Me: "When did you want to go …"

My friend: (awkward pause) "… get our nails done tomorrow."

Me: (rushing ahead) "… curtain shopping?"

Chapter 9

My friend: (awkward pause) "We could combine the two …."

Me: "for curtains."

My friend: (rushing ahead) "… if you'd like."

Me: "Why don't we go curtain shopping tomorrow." (thoughtful pause) "When should we get our nails done?"

Finally, I will repeat myself to emphasize a point. I don't trust you to recognize my vehemence unless I say the same thing two or three times. Flag waving and inspirational background music are also acceptable. I just want to be sure my kids are not showing their good manners by ignoring me.

Name that old adage

Throughout the years, people have been using sayings as tools to remember life's important lessons. Ever notice how "a rolling stone gathers no moss" rarely comes up in casual conversation these days? This adage has been around for a long time, but I still can't fathom the depths of its inscrutability. There's something very Zen about moss on stones, so I'm thinking it is better not to roll them. Just remember, as you're adjusting the Feng Shui of your rock garden, not to let the grass grow under your feet.

Then you have vague and questionable comparisons:

A bird in the hand is worth two in the bush.

Better safe than sorry.

A stitch in time saves nine.

Who actually weighs these two possibilities when making a decision? Apparently, I do. I was recently trying to avoid an expensive trip to the veterinarian's. As I was spreading salve on my dog's boo-boo and wrapping his foot in a sandwich bag band-aid, I thought, "an ounce of prevention is worth a pound of cure." The phrase popped into my brain with the annoying spontaneity of a Barry Manilow song. Great, now I'm humming Copa Cabana while picturing my dog with a bag on his foot.

I'm embarrassed to say some adages from the stone age are still in my lexicon, like "too big for his britches." Obviously, pants are rarely referred to as "britches" in current jargon.

Here are some adjectives over the years meaning, "good":

The bee's knees *n* the joints between the femur and tibia of a hymenopterous insect

Swell *vb* to expand abnormally: to puff up due to internal pressure

Groovy *adj* having long narrow channels or depressions

Keen *adj* acute or astute

Chapter 9

The shit *n* bodily waste discharged through the anus
Phat *adj* opherweight.

One thing I've learned in life is that if you make hay while the sun shines, you obviously don't live in Seattle.

Advertising: the oldest form of pandering

Do you know how many times I go to the store to get bread and come home with everything but bread. Return to the store—repeat. If I didn't have advertising to remind me of all the things I can't live without, I might end up with nothing in my cupboards but dust rags and beef jerky.

In early television (in *our* day), Captain Kangaroo advertised products as part of the show. The FCC later ruled that Mr. Green Jeans would not be allowed to advise Bunny on the relative merits of one brand of corn flakes over another. When commercials could no longer be incorporated into scheduled programming, enter product placement. It's not advertising when a movie character spends thirty seconds on screen drinking a Yoo Hoo. It's OK to splatter an athlete's shorts with tampon brands. I was watching the Lakers last night and had a sudden urge to buy feminine hygiene products, even though I finished menopause several years ago.

One of the most subtle forms of advertising is subliminal BUY MY BOOK messages. Some commercials use phrases EVER LOVE A LAND ROVER? or celebrities with names similar to the product name. More insidious is the power of suggestion to actually spur GO TO THE BOOKSTORE NOW people to action. You must be ever vigilant EXCEPT THIS TIME to avoid this cheap attempt at persuasion.

Chapter 10
Young Whippersnappers

What would old age be without the opportunity to criticize young people? As long as our youth are texting behind the wheel, they are robbing old people of their God-given right to be the undisputed terrors of the interstate. The younger generation denies their children critical immunities by wiping out 99.9% of bathroom germs, and they couldn't crochet a doily if their lives depended on it. They believe they are entitled to instant gratification without putting in the time and labor. Perhaps it's our fault for not crushing their spirits with the harsh realities of life early on, but better late than never.

XYZ – What generation are we up to now?
As a generation, we have a cool name. Baby boomers—conceived during the post war (WWII) sigh of relief. We've seen Korea, Vietnam, and The Cold War. We've cheered, protested, and dived under our desks during

atomic bomb practice at school. If the big one hit, we probably wouldn't have been any better off because we knew how to duck and cover, but at least we knew every random wad of gum stuck to the bottom of our desks.

A generation is a rather exclusive club, limited to people born within a specific timeframe. We shared common perspective, soft drinks, and backwash. We ran the gamut from the Beatles to the Bee Gees; saw the birth of color television, and the streak. Every generation thinks theirs is the best. That's where all the other generations are wrong.

Who got to wear mini skirts to school? Everybody in my generation except me — at least that's what it seemed like. Who had love-ins, sit-ins and keggers? Again, not me — but that's not your fault; I totally blame my parents. We had Sunday drives in the family station wagon and family reunions. (Watch out for Uncle Stuart: he likes to pinch girls on the bottom). We had American Bandstand, and we had Dick Clark. OK, picking on Dick is just too easy, so insert your own Dick Clark joke here.[19] ___

Later generations can claim alternative rock and Hip Hop, but they didn't have Motown. Contemporary music pales next to Diana Ross and the Supremes. I was jealous

---

[19] Example: When other stars are having face-lifts, Dick Clark is having taxidermy.

Chapter 10

of my cousins because they had Diana's "Love Child" album. But I always felt sorry for the Pips. Whoever came up with that name should be forced to listen to a Polka music marathon.

I've never twittered, owned an iPod, or created a home page. It takes one to three minutes for me to send the text message: "OK." If information technology is the measuring stick of the current young generation, I'll take Goldie Hawn dancing in a bikini and psychedelic body paint every time. Our measuring sticks were less technical, but more fun.

Just text "**don't bother" to let me know which one you prefer.

What's left after we kill 99.9% of bathroom germs
I was not the first born in our family, so Mom didn't sterilize my nipples or pacifiers when I dropped them on the ground. There seemed little point since I ate my own poop as a baby. When I became a toddler, I switched my eating habits to banana slugs and dirt. As a young child, my sisters and I shared sandwiches, sodas, apples, and I ate my own boogers — and I turned out OK.

My grandmother got her water from the pump house that drew from the creek. When our Labrador retriever jumped into the creek, you could count on drinking mud and dog toe juice for the next 15 minutes. Grandma had a dipper hanging on the cabinet next to her sink. Rather than wash untold number of water glasses, we all drank from the communal dipper. I had to wait until my cousins gathered around the sink so that the tallest of them could fill the dipper for little old me. That meant that I got my dipper full of heavy metals and backwash after everyone else—and I turned out OK.

Mom told me not to touch dead birds because they had cooties, but I played with my pet rats, none of which ever got a bath. I didn't brush after every meal and I didn't wash my hands every time I peed. We had a large wooden slide-out cutting board, which was scarred and blistered and smelled vaguely of gym socks. It's where we cut meat, cleaned fish, rolled out dough, and made mud pies. We all shared a single bathroom—and ... you know the drill.

Modern mothers have created a monster. In trying to eradicate every speck of bacteria in their children's vicinity, germs have become so resistant it takes napalm and mustard gas to kill them. I blame advertising for creating this microbial mass hysteria. You just don't see cleaning products on TV without "anti-bacterial" on the label. If you want to sanitize the air you breathe, but pushing the button on a spray can is too hard, plug in a fresh scent with an automatic deodorizer. It is guaranteed

Chapter 10

to eradicate dust mites, dander, and nuclear fallout all day.

I don't have any statistics to show you, but I believe our exposure to bacteria, viruses and allergens when we were young toughened-up our immune systems. Nobody heard of flu shots when I was a kid. Heck, the oral polio vaccine was not invented until I was six years old.

We were oblivious to the dangers of exposure to the sun, asbestos, second hand smoke, high-tension power lines, and lead based paints. Instead, we were busy looking for a cure for the common cold, which is hardly a blip on the radar now. What's a little virus compared to flesh-eating bacteria?

Whatsoever you sew, so shall ye rip
You can tell a lot about a generation by their needlework skills. When my oldest daughter turned sixteen, she received a hope chest filled with yarn. She looked in the chest and began to cry; to my astonishment, they were not tears of joy. I guess she was hoping to find a pony inside. She probably should have been tipped off by the lack of air holes drilled in the sides.

When I was growing up, passing along the torch of needlework from grandmother, to mother, to child was a bonding experience, not unlike a fraternity hazing. Grandma taught me to knit slippers, embroider pillowcases, crochet lace, and regret my lineage. My mother helped me learn the intricacies of sewing Barbie clothes. This was the era in which we made or bought whole wardrobes for our *one* Barbie doll, which was bought wearing nothing but a one-piece bathing suit and impossibly high stiletto heels. By the way, what genius decided girls should learn how to sew by honing their skills on dresses with one-eighth inch seams, and buttons the size of baby fleas? But I digress.

So naturally, my choice for my daughter's coming of age was that we crochet a granny square afghan together. Once I taught her the basics and forced her help me finish the odious project, she began to regret her lineage.

I resolved never to impose my needlework expertise on my kids again, which is why I was amazed when the same child asked me to teach her to sew. It turns out she's very good at it, despite the legacy of shortcuts and bad habits, which my mother passed to me.

Most all of the young people I've polled on the subject do not have the rudimentary skills necessary to knit a sweater or crochet a doily (or even know what a doily is). They are as clueless with a sewing machine as I am at setting the radio station buttons in my car. You doubt the significance of needlework to the anthropological architecture of a society? Say that to big scary looking dude, Rosy Greer, who showed off his

Chapter 10

needlepoint projects on television talk shows years ago. He could give my grandma a run for her money.

That's entertainment

Back in my day, we wasted hours watching reruns on television. Now kids waste hours playing video games on computers, hand-held game systems, and even games on cell phones. Kennedy instituted the President's Council on Physical Fitness to make sure couch potatoes could play Jai Alai and bench press compact cars. It seems like we've lowered the bar a little. The latest program is the NFL's "Play 60," which encourages kids to get out of the house for at least sixty minutes a day to run around as if they had fire ants in their shorts.

I'm afraid our generation has to take some of the blame. Damn our high tech Atari systems, and killer games like "Asteroids" and "Pong!" We had all the thrill of making a smiley face eat fruit and ghosts. At least games now have a plot and movie-like quality. Of course, that only makes it harder to justify all the time I spent playing my low-tech "Space Invaders."

If you want to take your gaming to the next level, you can try out for *Survivor*. You don't see a whole lot of fifty-somethings on reality shows. Maybe they have a sign in casting that says, "You have to be this tall, stupid, or combative, to play." Maybe by our age we don't feel the need to demean ourselves on national TV. That doesn't stop us from watching young people humiliate themselves. Suddenly, playing "Space Invaders" doesn't sound so stupid.

I sometimes rue all the violence and gore in modern movies, until I remember we were the generation that went from cheesy science fiction to mutilation.

- 1973   The Exorcist (head-spinning fun)
- 1974   Texas Chainsaw Massacre
- 1978   Halloween
- 1979   The Amityville Horror
- 1980   Friday the Thirteenth

Even *Aliens* came out over 20 years ago, back when Sigourney Weaver had her original breasts. Modern moviemakers can't find subjects scary enough anymore, so they have to fall back on remakes of our horror films.

It makes it kind of hard to resent young whippersnappers for their entertainment that devalues humanity. Instead, I'll just have to resent the fact their axe-murderer movies have better special effects than ours did.

Stamp of approval

If you look at letters from teenage soldiers of the civil war, the writing looks like beautiful calligraphy with impeccable spelling. Letters were a lifeline to family and

Chapter 10

friends and were taken very seriously. They were saved and cherished for years.

Once a week like clockwork, my grandma sent us a letter. Once a week we learned more than we ever wanted to know about her sciatica and the weather in Naselle, Washington. Before the days of email, I wrote letters each week to grandmothers and parents. These were also the days in my young married life when I could buy a roll of one hundred stamps for $15.

Now the Post Office doesn't have the courage to print the postage amount on the face of the stamps or the booklet covers. What people don't realize is that postage, relative to the value of the dollar, has changed very little since the 1860's. The US Postal Service is barely keeping up with inflation — technically known as deep financial doo-doo.

Between texting and email, the first class letter is becoming extinct. My husband pays most of our bills online, so he doesn't even use the return envelopes provided with the bill. A packet of twenty stamps can last us six months.

This is supposed to be the part where I criticize young people because they do their correspondence in a haphazard manner, not giving a fig about punctuation, spelling, or grammar. They have texting shorthand that requires a degree in cryptology to crack. No longer satisfied with email, they send their 4G (whatever that means) messages via Facebook and such, where twittering is the name of the game. They are creating new words, like "unfriend". This is a checkbox to remove someone from "friend" status on your Facebook page.

Unfriend *verb*: a highly impersonal and cowardly method for ending a friendly relationship. *noun*: a person who has been unfriended, or who has initiated an unfriending

The truth is young people probably correspond far more than we did in letter writing days. What modern communication lacks in elegance, it makes up for in volume. I propose we as seniors blitz the postal system with real handwritten letters to the young people in our lives. We'll declare a national snail mail week in August, when other holidays are scarce and the TV stations are showing reruns. Everyone over 50 is required to write at least one letter each day of the week to a young person. You get extra points for using a fountain pen: points off for using college ruled notebook paper.

Write something your loved ones can save and cherish for years to come. There is no delete button on a handwritten letter, no spell and grammar check, nor any mailing groups. Before cursive becomes a lost language, let's share it with our kids and increase the Post Office's

Chapter 10

revenue. We can spawn a writing revolution, or at least get rid of seven stamps before the rates go up again.

Den of iniquity

If you can believe the polls, 40 percent of Americans attended church last Sunday. I was not one of them. Other than me, around 20 percent of Americans lie through their teeth. People exaggerate their charitable giving, voting record, and manly conquests. They play down their use of cocaine and Viagra . Of course, they're going to lie about church attendance, and go straight to Hell. Do not pass confession, do not collect absolution.

I was dragged to church services, Sunday school, and prayer meetings to give me a good background of moral and spiritual values, and so I could wear a lace doily on my head. I see fewer and fewer young families going to church. You only have to go to the local flea market on a Sunday morning to find the backsliders, Philistines, and heathens. Last week I found a 1929 copy of a National Geographic magazine at the market. I figure that's worth a little brimstone or a night of sleeping on bristle rollers.

Sense of entitlement quiz

Since I've never been published in Cosmopolitan, I will have to use this book to scientifically determine whether young people know the difference between privileges and rights.

Please answer the questions below as honestly as you can.

A. When your best friend gets a new outrageously expensive sports car from her dad, do you:
   1. Ask your dad for one
   2. Go into debt to buy one
   3. Wait until you're middle aged and go into debt to buy one
   4. Buy a 1975 Pacer for $50 and change

B. As soon as you graduate from college do you:
   1. Apply for the CEO position at a fortune 500 company
   2. Take over the family business
   3. Start in the mailroom of a business and work your way up
   4. Wash dishes at Herbert's Pancake Palace

C. Your political views on Medicare are:
   1. Do away with it completely. The senior citizens of this world are using up precious oxygen.
   2. Incorporate a "pull the plug" provision for any costly medical procedures
   3. The Medicare system is fine as it is

Chapter 10

    4. We've paid all our lives for Medicare benefits, so they should cover all health care needs

D. When confronted with an unexpected large expense, you:
   1. Ignore the bill
   2. Ask your parents for money
   3. Pay it in installments
   4. Dip into the money you've been setting aside for your knee replacement surgery

E. When examining your investment portfolio, you:
   1. Ask your parents to co-sign on a mortgage
   2. Look for a diversified investment strategy to minimize losses in an unstable economy
   3. Check for quarters under the sofa cushions
   4. Cry

F. When considering having children, do you:
   1. Get a playpen and a library of children's videos to entertain your baby while you're at work
   2. Expect your parents to provide free daycare
   3. Decide to wait until you are financially stable
   4. Thank God for menopause

G. When planning a vacation do you
   1. Crash at your parents' beach cottage for a few weeks
   2. Go into debt to stay at a tropical paradise

3. Go camping in the State Park
4. Save money all year to visit the potato museum in Idaho

Add the numbers of your answers from all questions.
If you score:
- 0 – 6   You seriously need a refresher course in testing instructions and basic math skills.
- 7 – 14   You are age 18 to 30 and believe the world owes you. The quicker you become disillusioned, the quicker you can start paying your dues.
- 15-21   You are age 31 to 45 and are beginning to recognize the harsh realities of adulthood. Hold onto the can-do attitude for as long as possible before you are swallowed up by crippling depression and alcoholism.
- 22-28   You are age 46 to 55, and your jaded outlook is looking for an escape through a mid-life crisis. Buy your sniper's rifle now for menopause.
- 29 - 35   You are age 56 and over, and are becoming an opinionated curmudgeon, all judgmental of anyone younger than you. It is your responsibility to keep younger

Chapter 10

generations from building undue self-esteem.

What's the matter with kids today?
If you fall into the judgmental curmudgeon category, you probably remember the line above from the movie, "Bye-Bye Birdie." It is a favorite subject for seniors and can occupy hours of Canasta conversation.

The major complaint is that kids want to earn more for doing less. We did our time flipping burgers at the malt shop, and pumping gas. We worked as bus-boys, waitresses, babysitters, and baggers. But young people these days eschew such plumb positions, or quit after two weeks.

I made fifty cents an hour babysitting, and once was paid a hamster. By the time I was looking for babysitters, I was desperate enough to pay five dollars an hour. I know I was getting ripped off, but I told myself my precious children were worth that much as I sprinted for the door. We've all had really bad jobs at one time or another, so we get pretty grouchy when our youth want to skip this important developmental step.

Is this our fault? Probably. We have fundamentally failed in our duty to crush their spirits. We have left our young people with a dangerously unrealistic sense of optimism. Young people these days *think* they know it all. Those of us in the mature age group *know* we know it all. The good news is that since youngsters don't listen to us, they can't see through our bull.

It's early yet, so we'll give the young people the benefit of the doubt. They are still deciding where their priorities lie, but then again, so are we.

Chapter 11
Dressing your Middle Age

For many years, I took my children's advice on fashion. I shopped in the juniors' department and bought skintight jeans that came nowhere near my belly button in the front, and far too close to my butt crack in the back. I was hanging on as long as I could to bikinis, but eventually, various body parts succumbed to gravity and started oozing out the bottom of both pieces. After menopause, most women have to trade in their two-piece bathing suits for something with a little skirt. When trying on clothes in general, you look in enough three-way mirrors that you decide the only way to draw people's attention away from your trouble spots is to set fire to the dressing room.

When you can't read the tag, it's time to get out of the juniors' department
When my daughters were in their teens, they decided to dress me like a Barbie doll. It became a horrible travesty

of a makeover show. They sent most of my clothes to Goodwill and deep-sixed every pair of granny panties in my drawer. Once I had little left to wear out of the house, they took me to the mall. I came home with two pairs of low-rise jeans which flashed the back of my new dental floss thong panties every time I sat down. I had a duty to my peers to prove we could pull off teenager chic. On the downside, I couldn't ignore the fact I was taking my fashion cues from people who had not yet attained legal drinking age. That ruled out the excuse that our wardrobe choices were a product of too many Margaritas.

My next natural step was to become a hypocrite. I began to look down my nose at those other middle-aged women who tried to rock the tight jeans. Any baby-boomer who didn't have a broad selection of relaxed-fit slacks in their closet was just trying to prove something. For my part, I would squeeze my ham-like thighs into narrow-leg jeans and smugly rejoice if there was no overt swooshing sound as I walked.

Preparing for shopping was getting to be a military operation. God forbid somebody saw my feet under the dressing room door and notice a bunion. Before shopping I would:

- ✓ Dye gray roots
- ✓ Remove all telltale corn pads

Chapter 11

- ✓ Put on an extra support bra
- ✓ Exfoliate and moisturize
- ✓ Apply concealer and make-up.

All good things must come to an end. You can hide a lot of things with make-up, but hands can be a dead giveaway. When you're holding a short pleated schoolgirl skirt in hands covered in protruding veins, ropy tendons, and liver spots, the game is up. Imagine my surprise when my fellow juniors began to sneer at me each time I entered the dressing rooms. Kids can be cruel.

One thing the juniors' department lacks is clothing for hot flashes. Obviously, the clothing manufacturers didn't think that one through. I've become very conscious of layering my clothes since the onset of menopause, since I chill easily between hot flashes. Dressing in a lightweight half-length Miley Cyrus vest might look hot, but it's not going to keep me hot. Mid-life layering is all or nothing. You need to start with pasties and a G-string, proceed through turtleneck and nerdy sweater vest, and end with a down comforter.

I have since moved on to a store that does not even have a junior's department. The jeans are relaxed fit and all the skirts fall low enough to hide camel kneecaps. Sweaters have bright colorful patterns and t-shirts are strictly forbidden. I'd like to think that the clothes are youthful middle-age chic, and they make me look like a top mid-life model, but they aren't and they don't. Even so, since dressing this *cool* costs a small fortune, I'm never letting my kids near my closet again.

Bathing suits are from the devil

I wonder if we should go back to the days of bathing dresses. Just look at any tabloid at the checkout stands and you'll see that even the most beautiful people cannot hide their varicose veins and cellulite in a bikini. The whole idea behind the bikini was to attract guys and minimize tan lines. That in itself should be a red flag to seniors who are considering reliving their youthful beach look. The reason this ill-conceived plan won't work is:

a. Guys aren't attracted to the aforementioned varicose veins and cellulite
b. Tan lines are the only "safe zones" from melanoma left on your body. No point in making your sunscreen put in overtime
c. Wearing figure-flattering clothes only works if you're wearing clothes.

Before our first bikinis, we wore a *two-piece*. There is a major distinction. While a bikini covers just enough skin to prevent beach pornography (definition: I'll know it when I see it), the two-piece had big enough bottoms to cover our backsides without any rolls peeking out, and the top had a bra with actual cups instead of triangular

Chapter 11

scraps of fabric. Once you find the coveted "perfect" two-piece bathing suit, you will wear it to every beach and pool party for the next three to seven years. You know the elastic has lived a full and happy life when the top drags down to your belly and your bottoms end up around your ankles each time you dive in headfirst. I tried to be aware of any textured surface I sat on, but the bottoms still turned to cheesecloth, right on the edge of obscene, before I retired my favorite white two-piece.

Enter the senior one-piece. The days of wearing a two-piece and keeping a bikini hidden in the bottom of my drawer are gone. But even as I admit fashion defeat, a new challenge arises: camouflage. It could be built-in cups for the sagging bosom, corset strength Lycra for the tummy, or a "little skirt" to hide the tush and hips. Are dark colors more slimming? Does a print or pattern break up the profile? Is a beach cover an accessory or a courtesy to others?

Since they don't have real people modeling bathing suits, I have to look at half-starved models in a catalogue when making my choice. I could go to the store and actually try stuff on, but other people have had their privates pressed against the same piece of fabric that would be digging into mine. So I look at a model who is six inches taller than me and half my weight. If a swimsuit looks great on her, it should accomplish my goal of not looking freakishly bad on me. I'll let you know when I find it.

When all is said and done, there are many seniors who look beautiful in a bathing suit, but I don't seem to be one of them. Maybe if I had the perfect suit, the right lighting, a good camera filter, and a team of air-brushers, I could look as good as a swimsuit model.[20]

Shorts + Wicker = Chenille marks

OK, I get it. As we get older our skin loses elasticity. You push two solid masses together, and the squishier one is going to give first, often oozing into each nook and cranny of the firmer surface. That was fine when I was a thirteen year-old gymnast with thighs like granite — not as much 40+ years later on those days when oxygen feels firmer than my thighs.

Years ago, bathrobes and bedspreads were often made of a soft white material decorated with nubs, like little knots lined up into patterns. The problem with the chenille bedspread was that if you tried to sneak a nap, you'd wake up with drool on your pillow and telltale indentations on your face. Chenille may be a thing of the past, but sagging skin is not.

As long as we have to think of summer sooner or later, let us remember these simple senior fashion rules:

---

[20] If she's wearing a burka

Chapter 11

Shorts + wicker = chenille marks

Be aware of the location of your thighs at all times. Grass, towels, and most lawn furniture is going to leave a mark. Resist the urge to sit down until after dark.

Sun + skin = age spots

The same sun that used to give you a glowing tan will now give your face all the luster of a Guernsey cow (brown and white spots, for those of you not born in a barn). Once mother nature has blotched up your skin, it will take faithful use of sunscreen, expensive cosmetics, and the rest of your life to unblotch.

Bathing suit + middle age spread = disaster

I haven't had the courage to go bathing suit shopping yet. I'm thinking there is no day so hot I am willing to bare that much doughy skin in public. Even trying on a one-piece is going to require panels, Lycra, and a bottle of lighter fluid, so if necessary, I can set fire to the dressing room to draw the eye away from my trouble spots.

Walk-in wonderland

Rubbermaid tubs in the garage, under-bed storage containers, spare room closet, space bags (as seen on TV) … I've tried a lot of things to conveniently transfer my winter clothes into storage during the summer, and vice versa. Let me assure you, there's nothing "convenient" about sucking the air out of a bag with a vacuum. Once inside, your clothes are lost in the black hole of "too hard." My quandary: I would rather gargle with drain cleaner than go shopping, but I would rather chew broken glass covered in Tabasco sauce than have to re-inflate and deflate the same bag over and over, just to get out my argyle socks with the tassels.

Shuffling under-bed boxes isn't much easier. Only the footboard has enough clearance to get the boxes in and out. Suddenly you're on your belly playing a cramped game of Tetris, with game pieces stuffed full of souvenir sweatshirts from your trip to Couer d'Alene, Idaho. Game over!

A few years ago, as our house was being built, we went to oversee various stages of its construction. One of the most exciting trips was when they had just put the hardware into the walk-in closet. There were so many shelves! I had more wire racks of wonderfulness than I could ever possibly use. There was even room for t-shirts that said, "I'm with Stupid," and blue flannel pajamas covered in pink flamingos.

I had a shelf where my only hat would be safe from the crush of unfinished embroidery projects. There was room for the unmarked shoebox hiding my self-pleasuring appliance. I had two heights of bars and shelves on one wall—double decker storage at my finger tips. Instead, my sweatshirts and flannel jammy bottoms

Chapter 11

languish year around on the bottom shelf, while the top shelf sits empty, because if you have to pull out a step stool, you may as well be wrestling with under-bed containers.

Years ago, as a Navy wife, I would move at least every three years. It turns out that this was the only way I knew how to clean my closets. Now, my open-toe pumps with ankle laces sit unused ever since my ankles started oozing out the cracks. They lie next to the slippers that were partially eaten by the dog. He had blue poop for three days. For each move, I would sort through my stuff and heartlessly rid myself of the too-small slacks that used to look amazing on me, and the Christmas socks printed with festive smiling clams.

We would like to retire and grow old in our current house, but my closet is starting to look like a museum. I'd hate to move just to get rid of my skinny jeans. That would be even harder than space bags.

Guess your dress size
Women's sizes have always been a little subjective. Different manufacturers seem to produce clothes for women from different planets. I have the same ham-like thighs that I had in college, but I wear a dress three sizes smaller than I did then. In the really expensive lines (unusual for my budget), I can fit into outfits up to five

sizes smaller than I wore in college. It turns out you *can* put a price on vanity.

Manufacturers have figured out that a woman who eats Cheetos for lunch wants to feel good about her appearance, the same as someone who eats butterfly wings. If we can't budge the extra pounds with protein water and 10-minute workouts, the next best thing is to change the labels on the clothing.

In college, I weighed less than I do today, I had two pairs of size 14 jeans, and I thought I looked smokin' hot. Today I weigh twenty pounds more and have two pairs of size 10 jeans, and I think I look five months pregnant. As I said, I am now shopping in a grown-up clothing store, so the sizing is especially forgiving.

I don't want to take anything away from women who have successfully lost weight. You have to defy the odds to really lose weight and keep it off. My hat is off to you! I would also encourage women to find the size that's right for *them*. Many women look and feel great in a size 14. You go, girls!

To be honest, the only reason I'm whining is because if I could be sure that a size 10 on a shopping website would fit, I would never darken the doors of an actual fitting room again. Hell, if a clothing delivery truck crashed into my living room, I'm not sure I could be bothered to try on clothes before deciding what to loot.

Chapter 11

While we are feeling better about our clothing sizes, the seniors in advertising tend to look younger and more fit than the average fifty or sixty year-old real life woman: certainly more than me. They probably wear size 2. We just can't get a break!

That dress looks familiar
Have you ever been in this position? You show up at a party and someone is wearing the same dress as you. You both feel awkward knowing that you hit the same sale at Target. Hers is probably a size 2, and yours is not.

What if you get a one-of-a-kind handmade dress from Goodwill and the next month your boss' wife says, "I used to have a dress just like that." It's happened to me, and it's one of those awkward moments from which there is no graceful exit. My usual response to embarrassing situations is to stammer incomprehensibly. Now I have an obvious hand-me-down and a speech impediment. Perfect!

When I was growing up, my grandma would frequently make three identical dresses for my sisters and me. One particular set had beautiful hand smocking on the bodice, but I could see the underlying truth: grandma hated nonconformity.

Since then, I've had children of my own and have discovered the joy of recycled clothing. Mothers of young, rapidly growing children understand that going green means keeping perfectly good leotards out of landfill. Adults are not exempt from recycling; I've also reaped the rewards of other people's weight gains or losses.

"Look at these amazing jeans I found at the thrift store." I enthused. "They put the decorative slit on the inside of the trouser leg by mistake, but it still has the price tag on it. I guess someone was overly optimistic about getting into a size 6."

"I didn't know you wore a size 6," my friend said skeptically.

"I will after my new diet. You lose 20 pounds in three weeks eating nothing but Snickers bars."

"That sounds amazing! Would you consider passing the jeans on to me when you give up on a size six? I should have lost 20 pounds by then on my pasta and Fritos diet."

I see London, I see France
Women's panty sizes are another humiliating experience. No two booties are the same, yet underwear comes in approximately four sizes. My hip circumference is about the same as my daughter's, but the same panties that fit her hips strain to keep my fleshy derriere inside. From the back I ooze out the bottom like a really disturbing

Chapter 11

Salvador Dalí painting. If bras can have a cup size, why can't panties have a cheek size?

Of course, that would not be an issue if we all wore thong underwear. Then the only problem would be a world full of women so cranky that Manolo Blahniks would have to come with a warning label:

> "Not responsible for kicking injury done to cuddly innocent puppies as a result of wearing these shoes while operating thong underwear."

It would make a man remember fondly the days when his woman was premenstrual, but wearing granny panties. Even now, I believe that when registering for a handgun, a woman should have to declare if she wears a thong — in the interest of full disclosure.

A variety of "rises" to slacks and jeans is no longer reserved exclusively for the juniors' department. Women's jeans now need corresponding underwear. Goodbye granny panties, hello day of the week bikini underwear. Currently, Wednesday through Saturday are in the wash.

In a perfect world, panties would come high enough to cover stretch marks, while low enough to cover cellulite. I'm sure that knee length panties (with cheek sizes) will catch on soon.

Whatever the occasion, there is never so much dirty laundry that you should ever be tempted to wear your husband's underwear! Nothing says more clearly, "I have lost the will to live" than a woman in tighty whities.

Throughout your adult life, you have maintained two sets of panties: period underwear and everyday underwear. Once a pair of panties gets stretched out, the elastic gets broken, or they develop a hole, they go into the period undie pile. Menopause brings its share of inconveniences and problems, but we can celebrate the one positive change. Like a coming of age ceremony, I believe women should invite their friends for a period panty bonfire. Just stand far enough back from the flames if you are having a hot flash.

I didn't get the muumuu memo

I have a small waistline … relative to a land mass the size of Pangea just south of the belt border. With a gut in the front, and a very generous booty in the back, it's hard to find a dress that doesn't breathe a sigh of relief when it goes from the dressing room to the rack of shame. Let's just say I'm not a stranger to the sound of popping threads when I'm trying on clothes. I tend to be ~~delusional~~ overly optimistic when selecting a dress.

I love wearing sundresses in the summer. The feel of fabric swishing around my legs … the ventilation … the

Chapter 11

lack of discernible shape. I'm starting to see the benefits of the muumuu: a dress originated in Hawaii for women with the physique of a sumo wrestler on steroids. I'm not alone in this regard.

Walking through the Uber-Mart the other day, I noted that the muumuu was a popular fashion decision. Uber-Mart has a strict dress code. Tuesdays are jeans skirt days, and for those of us who cannot find industrial strength double stitching, Thursdays are muumuu days. I didn't get the memo, so it was quite by accident that I found myself in fashion compliance last week.

The advantages of a muumuu in Uber-Mart are obvious. You can scratch your back against a freezer door handle without attracting undue attention. (Those things are awesome back scratchers). Disadvantages: a very cold breeze on your lady parts when climbing up the shelves of said freezer to get the last stuffed portabella mushroom Lean Cuisine.

Traditionally, a muumuu should have enough fabric to house a family of four. I'm proud to say mine could only sleep two midgets and a wet golden retriever comfortably. (My apologies in advance to any Hawaiians for this unfortunate stereotype). I don't wear leis, play the ukulele, or wail out songs that sound like there's a gopher in heat nearby. My muumuus aren't printed with flowers the size of mini-vans. Still, I want to thank the

Hawaiians for this ugly yet functional piece of apparel. I just wish they would call it something that doesn't sound like a herd of Holsteins. There's no need to point out the correlation between cows and my figure.

Socks and underwear Christmas

Every year I tell my children that if they are particularly naughty, or if we are particularly broke, the sock fairy will visit our house instead of Santa Claus. I was brainwashed in my youth to think panties had to be white and bras were either white, black or beige. The first year I got matching bra and panties for Christmas I was sold. I asked the sock fairy to come to my house every Christmas and birthday so I could wear matching underwear every day. It was a stupid little victory in life, but I went from new perky breasts to an old sagging bosom before I actually got a pretty bra. The sock fairy owed me.

This last birthday, I asked for the usual gifts. When I opened the first box and found it was the wrong kind of bra, I was crushed. Anyone with tennis ball-in-tube-socks breasts knows exactly what I'm talking about. If the senior breast is not supported properly, there is a large chasm between the top edge of the bra and the skin, leaving a tell-tale line under your shirt. I thought a smaller bra would be the answer, but I'm still banned

Chapter 11

from the junior department. Next year, I'll just buy my own underwear and talk to the Gucci fairy.

What goes around comes around
A woman in the grocery store parking lot recently commented that my skirt looked like something from 30 years ago. Actually, I'm rather proud of my vintage style clothing. You won't find a stitch of polyester anywhere in my closet.[21] I had worn this particular skirt for thirty years because it was Pendleton wool from Oregon. Yes, Oregon produces some very fine things besides beaver pelts and cheese.

I also have a thirty year-old lambskin jacket that would have PETA members storming my house with torches and pitchforks. I've never been a slave to style. Once I find something that flatters my figure, it becomes a permanent resident in my closet, where it gets lots of love and attention.

"That's a lovely suit." Lori remarked.

"Thank you," I said. "It's wool, so it's pretty hot, and the pant legs are unlined and scratchy since it was made during the Civil War era. I wouldn't be surprised if they made it out of a horse blanket, but the cut makes my waist look tiny."

---

[21] I think I mentioned I'm a shameless liar

matronly *adj* having the characteristics of a married woman marked by dignified maturity

Just the suggestion of the word evokes an old black and white photograph of your Great Aunt Tilly in a dark colored dress with a lace collar. Add a string of pearls and you have the whole picture.

Why do we automatically associate "dignified maturity" with frumpy? Because I can't imagine supermodels on a Paris runway dressing like Ethel Mertz from *I Love Lucy*. While June Cleaver was rocking the housedress, poor Ethel had to wear oversized floral print (yawn) granny dresses. It was never haute couture; now it's a Halloween costume.

In the 60's, fashion was all about being "mod." Do you think go-go boots and micro mini-skirts might one day be considered "matronly?" After all, our grandchildren would consider them a Halloween costume.

The point is that whatever you are wearing at this very moment qualifies as "matronly." Look in the mirror—this is what your grandchildren do NOT want to look like. Your paisley blouse and pleated slacks are the current frumpy dark dress with lace collar. If you don't own a string of pearls, you should really get on that.

Chapter 12
Exploring New In-Continents

No book can do justice to the vast number of human indignities associated with aging. While we're gaining weight, we're losing hair, and bladder control. Costly dental work is the payback for lack of good oral hygiene in our youth. There are too many anal embarrassments to detail. We can go from top to bottom—bifocals to bunions, and only scratch the surface. More advanced indignities are beyond the scope of this course.

Depends on how you spell it
Dignity is highly overrated. Sure, it's nice to be able to hold your head up in public, but for me that ship has sailed.

Any woman who has pooped out a baby has had her pelvic sling muscles stretched like a sweater on Jane Mansfield. You have experienced how laughing, coughing, jumping, or running could spell disaster for your underwear and your self-esteem.

I kegeled my heart out, but to no avail, so I went to the urologist to talk about my little problem. In the waiting room they had a fountain, a picture of a waterfall, and a CD playing the sounds of nature; it was a babbling brook with the haunting beauty of a flushing toilet. I think it was supposed to be restful, but the women in line for the bathroom didn't look too rested.

Incontinence is a serious matter, which happens to be funny. I may not be in kindergarten, but there is no expiration date on potty humor. One minute I was laughing, and the next I was crying because I had peed my pants.

I started with panty liners and moved up to maxi pads. I got to a point where my only options were surgery or diapers. I figured that diapers would be bulky, smelly and landfill unfriendly. I was also pretty sure I would rather be covered with fire ants than carry a package of adult diapers to the checkout stand in Uber-Mart. I opted for surgery.

Now I can stop the flow when I want to, or when I don't want to. I can pee sideways without even trying, but my panties and bank account are dry.

That's just peach-fuzzy!
If individual body parts can get dementia, I believe hair is the first to go. As we age, it starts growing in all the

Chapter 12

wrong places in a mass migration from our heads. Androgenetic alopecia is pattern baldness caused by the body's sensitivity to androgens (male hormones) on scalp hair follicles. The pattern tends to be different for women than for men, but the cause is the same.

Women just have to accept that as the lady hormones go, the mustache comes. I have one whisker which grows in the middle of my neck. Since it's hidden under my chin from my vantage point in the mirror, I have to do some difficult yoga positions to see it. Needless to say, I don't. Instead I cling to the perverse hope that this time will be different. Maybe the last plucking was so traumatic that the beardlet decided not to grow back. Imagine my surprise and horror when I see one strand of hair hanging down two inches from below my chin! An author is allowed a little license to exaggerate. Sadly, this is not one of those times.

Normally I stay at whatever cheesy motel will allow my bad puppies. Last year I had the opportunity to stay in a fancy hotel that left a morning newspaper at your door. There were plush bathrobes in the closet, and did I mention the newspaper? In the bathroom was a lighted mirror with a magnifier on one side. I took one look in the mirror and dashed down to the gift shop panting, "Tweezers, I need tweezers!"

Now I take my bathrobe, tweezers and a lighted mirror to every low brow motel where I stay, but I really miss the newspaper.

Cindy Crawford has nothing to worry about
Back when I was concerned about my appearance, I had a scale and weighed myself first thing each morning. I was careful to relieve myself and get on the scale naked to get the most accurate weight. I don't have a scale in my home anymore so I use the blue jeans test, graded as follows:

- A Baggy butt
- B Can pull waist band far enough out to see some daylight between jeans and stomach
- C Comfortable fit
- D Muffin top, camel toe, and inability to bend over
- F Need a can of shortening, a pair of pliers and a rosary to get into jeans

For years I could eat what I wanted, when I wanted, and not gain weight, because I only ate when I was hungry, and ate just enough to be satisfied. When I tried to dispense this advice to others struggling with their weight, they didn't exactly leap on the bandwagon like Elvis on a Twinkie.

Now that the metabolism is slowing down, my blue jeans test needs to be graded on a curve. When I weighed in at the doctor's office last week, I had gained ten pounds. I'm sure my shoes weighed at least three pounds. Without a scale of my own, I was forced to weigh myself at the drugstore. For some reason, when I did my usual pee and get on the scale naked routine, management got a little testy.

Bionic body parts
Once the warranty on your body expires, you will start to see attrition on the chassis and under the hood.

It doesn't seem fair. I didn't listen to heavy metal as a teen, and I don't go clubbing, but I'm reading lips more often than I used to. Prepare to rock the supertronic hearing enhancement look so you can hear a pin drop from Mexico.[22] Who wouldn't want to hear their kids whining in the next county?

When I was in third grade, a dentist came in to talk about the proper way to brush. He had a giant pair of choppers for his demonstration, and stroked them slowly and methodically with his giant brush. We were then forced to chew little red pills to show where we had missed the boat on oral hygiene. Despite this frightening display of the evils of plaque, I continued in my carefree dental lack of hygiene. Consequently, I got to make regular trips to the dentist for fillings. Note that dentists

---

[22] As seen on TV

didn't wear rubber gloves back then. My dentist smoked cigars, and when he stuck his hands in my mouth (which is conveniently located beneath my nose) I had to work not to gag.

Because of the sins of my youth, I had to get my first crown when I was thirty. Perhaps Dr. Giant Toothbrush could have mentioned molars composed of giant fillings have a shelf-life of approximately 20-30 years. I once broke a tooth on a banana, and I have to remember which side of my mouth to chew on when eating gummy bears.

When dentists tell you that you need a "procedure," just open your wallet and close your eyes. What they mean is they will create an artificial shell to surround what's left of your tooth. This crown will enable you to shell out vast sums of money to pay for institutes of higher learning for the dentist's children. Most parents these days are more strict about enforcing oral hygiene for their children. So if the baby boomers are the last generation of dental neglect, dentists' children will soon be panhandling on the corner of Third and Pine. It is the circle of life.

Back in the day, people could predict the weather through the aches in their joints. Rheumatism was frequently more dependable than meteorology. In an agrarian society, you depended on the Farmer's Almanac and Aunt Betsy's arthritis to get the hay in. This was

Chapter 12

especially important in the Seattle area, where I grew up. Making hay while the sun shone required split second timing.

Enter the era of hip replacement surgery. When I hear "prosthetics", I have an unfortunate picture of Captain Hook if he had a hook *and* a peg leg. Whether it is limb replacement or joint replacement, the science of prosthesis has added immense quality of life. Joint replacement is still relatively new. Most baby-boomers were in their teens or twenties in 1971, when the first total knee replacement surgery was performed on Horace Ledbetter's right knee. Unfortunately, it was the left kneecap that was blown. No longer just knees and hips, surgery can include shoulders, wrists, ankles or knuckles.

It's a good thing that meteorology has also seen advancements since the days of Aunt Betsy, or we'd be up to our ears in wet hay!

Don't cut the cheese, please
Gas is about simple mathematics. The more you poop, the less you bloat. The more you age, the less you poop. As thoughtful senior citizens, we have a responsibility to the public to curtail our holiday festivities. Avoid corned beef and cabbage on St. Patrick's day, refried beans on Cinco de Mayo, and deviled eggs at the fourth of July cookout. The adult colon was not made to withstand the

onslaught of lactose intolerance or hummus. (They're practically interchangeable.)

If the Inuits have twenty different words for snow, adolescents have at least as many terms for gas. Southern Belles of a gentler era announced they had the vapors. Later generations politely ignored one another's gas in the same manner in which they kept their skeletons in the closets. Miss Manners would be proud.

When Grandma would literally putter around the house, we managed to giggle silently. We were raised to respect our elders, but kids these days don't seem to feel the need to revere those older and wiser and gassier than themselves. They unabashedly point out the obvious in loud and derisive terms, while we politely blame it on the dog. One day the kids will be old and gassy, and find themselves the butt of juvenile jokes. They will loudly proclaim, "Bad puppy!" It is the circle of life.

Straining the bounds of good taste
The most common causes of constipation are: insufficient water or fiber in your diet, certain medications, polyps or diverticulitis in the colon, hormone changes, slowed peristalsis related to aging, hemorrhoids, and the overuse of laxatives. We are so screwed.

Thank goodness for Jamie Lee Curtis. First of all, why would any celebrity want to be the poster child for

Chapter 12

irregularity? Secondly, she's pitching the bacterial fermentation of milk—way to sell it. On the upside, yogurt is benign for those who are mildly lactose intolerant. Jamie Lee's brand contains "secret ingredients" which help to regulate digestion: code for "helps you poop".

My grandmother made the Finnish version—viili. Viilia is yogurt with an added yeasty fungus culture on the surface. Yum! I couldn't even watch her eat this clabbered milk treat. Viilia was not for the faint of heart or the lactose intolerant. It tasted sour, and had the consistency of mucous. I'd like to see Jamie Lee try to sell that. But I digress.

When I was a kid, we had a hot water bottle with a hose and two different nozzles. These were designed to fit "comfortably" into two different human orifices. *Please don't mix up the nozzles!* The only advantage of this system over the disposable version is that you can put warm water into the hot water bottle. When you're shooting liquids up your behind, comfort is everything.

Even encyclopedias and dictionaries shy away from this procedure. When I looked up "enema" on the internet, it immediately asked if I meant to search for "enemy." I couldn't even find "colonic" in the dictionary. Spell check is currently trying to change the word to "colony."

Besides the obvious medical uses of the enema, the internet lists recreational uses right next to punitive uses. I can't even picture the first, and I shudder to think of the second. Either way, I'm going to have nightmares tonight.

Pain in the butt

No list of embarrassing body functions would be complete without the hemorrhoid. Like belly buttons, you can have inies or outies. Either way, they can ruin your day, week, or longer. When I itch, there is frequently a disconnect between my brain and my hand. I will suddenly find my hand in a place where I did not consciously send it. This is only a problem if you are:

- At a fancy dinner party
- Accepting the Nobel Peace Prize
- On a crowded bus
- At a job interview
- On a nationally televised cooking show.

Frequent hemorrhoid sufferers have perfected the art of sitting on one butt cheek, but it is hard to look dignified when you are constantly listing to the right.

It all comes down to a pooping Catch 22. You're damned if you doo and damned if you don't.

Diarrhea = hemorrhoids

Constipation = hemorrhoids

Chapter 12

Holding it = Septic shock and certain death

The best way to avoid the "roid" is fiber and fluids. Once one appears, there are over the counter ointments to ease the pain and itch. There is no known cure for the wandering hand associated with hemorrhoids. I suggest you turn down any invitation to compete on *Dancing with the Stars*. Len Goodman will mark you down for scratching.

Paul's Bunion

There has never in my life been a time when I thought my feet were cute. After the baby stage, nobody's feet are cute (unless you have a strange fetish). So why do women insist on wearing strappy sandals, long after the emergence of bunions and hammertoes? My baby toes look like big pink balls without toenails, trying to hide behind their next-door toe neighbors. Not attractive.

Women swear pencil-tip pointy shoes are comfortable. They lie. Does this shoe look remotely the same shape as your foot? Do you ever see them in wide widths? I've worn enough high heels, platform shoes, and clogs to bend my toes in ways God never intended. The rule of thumb is, the uglier the shoe, the better it is for your feet.

I'm not Imelda Marcos, but I was surprised to find twenty-five pairs of shoes and four pairs of boots in my closet. The thing is, I normally only wear one particular pair of shoes, one pair of boots, and one pair of slippers. The other twenty-two pairs of footwear sit pining away on the shoe rack waiting for me to don the one outfit they match. With their luck, that outfit is probably in my overly optimistic section of the closet.

There's no denying high heels make your legs and butt look great, but displays at a shoe store use size 5. The same shoes in a size 9 ½ might look like Cadillacs. You should avoid shoes that make you tower over your man, which leaves many women unable to wear heels at all. And the aforementioned pencil toe shoes make your feet look bigger than they already are, like a parody of Bozo the clown. Just ask my family how much I dislike clowns.

Eventually, women's shoes take their toll. Going to the foot care section of the department store has become a cloak and dagger operation. I look thoughtfully at Dr. Scholl's insoles until there is nobody in the aisle, before I swoop in and grab the corn pads. I make sure the self-check lanes are open, so the cashier doesn't see my shame. If anyone gets too close at checkout, I abort the mission, throwing the box in between cigarette lighters and gum next to the register.

Chapter 12

The eyes have it

I enjoyed 20/20 vision all my life, until I turned 42. That's when the first hint of problems began. Reading material was moving farther away from my face, and I was squinting a lot more. Reading for long periods would cause headaches and double vision. Inevitably, I got my first pair of reading glasses, so I would have something to leave on other people's desks, and an excuse to wear an ugly beaded idiot chain around my neck. The latter just succeeded in getting my glasses scratched up, smudged, and ridiculed.

Ten years later, I got my first set of bifocals. That's when I felt officially "old". Since then, I've started developing cataracts. That's when I felt officially sorry for myself. I think of people not blessed with perfect vision for most of their lives. Nope ... I still feel whiny and depressed about my vision.

My sister wore "hard" contacts when they first came out. They were pieces of glass, and she put them *in her eyes*. This required touching her eyes ... with her fingers!

God bless those brave enough to get corrective laser surgery. I think I'd have to have cataracts hanging out before I could consider someone getting close to my eyes with a laser or a knife. I expect I'll be wiping smudges off my bifocals for a long time to come, but I'm not going back to the idiot chain.

Chapter 13
I Shop but I'd Rather Drop

I don't shop the way I used to. Now I carry my cloth bags into the store, so I can throw my nice green groceries into the back of my gas-guzzler for the long drive home. That's not exactly true, because now I have to ask for help out to my car! Let me clarify: if I have to lift a bag of cat litter out of a cart, there will be crying involved. Now I point and click as much of my shopping as possible, from the comfort of my office chair. I might be eating cheese and salami gift boxes for dinner, but it keeps me out of the store.

Bag lady
Teddy Roosevelt created five National Parks in order to preserve wilderness areas for future generations. The baby-boomers did their part by chaining themselves to trees or dumping sugar into the gas tanks of bulldozers. After many years of letting somebody else worry about the environment, I've finally joined the ranks of boomer consumers who are concerned about either choking the landfills with disposable diapers, or finding their Uber-

Chapter 13

Mart bag in some random sperm whale's stomach. Either way, I don't think I would be able to sleep at night.

Like literally tens of others, I have opted for the reusable cloth bag approach. I feel a little conspicuous when I'm the only one walking into the store with cloth bags. Don't these people know about global warming? Are they totally indifferent to the plight of baby polar bears?

I actually dream of riding my bike or walking to the store. I see myself with my little folding grandma cart, two-wheeling my groceries home in their cloth bags. I'm not taking any moral high ground. I just need the exercise and have no shame. It could only be cooler if I wore curlers to the store.

For now, I load my cloth bags into my gas guzzling truck and drive eight miles to the nearest grocery store. If I want to save gas, I make my shopping part of my 30-mile one-way commute from work. I travel alone, so as not to inconvenience other people who don't want to stop for mayonnaise and hamburger buns on their way home.

You too can be environmentally aware. Do it for the whales.

Clipping coupons
As a young wife and mother, I wouldn't dream of going to the store without clipping coupons. It was just the socially acceptable thing to do. Gradually, people started

lining birdcages with the coupon section of the local paper. As money gets tight and the market keeps chewing away at people's retirement savings, I see more and more coupons directly in front of me in the grocery line.

With bar codes now printed on them, it should be an easy process to scan Mrs. Calloway's 78 coupons quickly, but something invariably goes wrong.

"I'm sorry ma'am. This coupon is only good for the 32-ounce size of Dustbuster Plus. You have the 24 ounce size." The cashier announces the inconsistency in a bored tone.

"How about I put back the Dustbuster Plus and get a second box of Chocolate Frosted Zombies? It comes with a half gallon of free milk."

"Your Dusbuster plus coupon is only good until the end of the week, but double coupon Wednesday is tomorrow."

"So I can get two half gallons of free milk tomorrow?" Mrs. Calloway's face is full of hope.

"You'll have to put your Chocolate Frosted Zombies back and buy two boxes at the same time tomorrow to get the milk."

"I'll just get my calculator for a moment. Let's put back all eighteen items with a coupon, and the box of Zombies, and I'll come back for them tomorrow."

"I'll have to call the supervisor."

Chapter 13

By now, I have finished reading about President Obama's love child and Oprah's latest heartache. I am resisting the urge to poke my eyes out with the ChapStick, but death by chocolate is looking highly appealing.

Store brand discount cards have been my substitute for the coupon hassle for many years. I've actually caught myself thinking about coupons recently. If I clip coupons *and* use my discount card, it will be like double coupon Wednesday every day! I can save up for a tube of ChapStick from the checkout line.

Would you like help out to your car?
I always cheerfully answered, "no thanks." I didn't need help, but it was nice to be asked. Now that I wouldn't mind some help, nobody's asking. I'm sure it's still part of a bagger's job description, but I feel a little awkward petitioning for assistance. I guess I should be flattered I don't look like I'm going to have a coronary before I reach the door.

First, asking for help is an admission of weakness, and the alpha wolf will eat the weakest members of the pack. It's a dog-eat-dog world.

Second, I hate begging for anything, especially when some 17 year-old with an iPod and no customer service skills resents having to heft my cat litter into the car. I don't have much patience for attitude.

Last week, I had to make a special shopping trip. By special, I mean making purchases that will put me into traction faster than I can wrestle an empty cart out of the pile. I wouldn't recommend saving all your bulky and heavy items for a single shopping trip. I had to double hand the 20-pound turkey and the 25-pound kitty litter. Add to that two 24-can cases of soda and a 12-pack of paper towels. When I made it home, I had to take four aspirins and a quart of raspberry sherbet.

I have reached that magical point when if I'm ever asked if I need help, I'm ready to swallow my pride and say, "Yes, please." My cervical vertebrae will thank me in the morning. I just have to watch out for parking lot wolves.

La-Z-Boy shopping

I think I've done my time. All my life, if I've needed to buy something, it has involved leaving the house and entering a store. Online shopping combines all the pleasure of not having to find a mall parking spot on Black Friday, with the adventure of being able to exceed my credit card's maximum balance in my underwear.

A little known fear related to agoraphobia is storeaphobia. It's not about the departure; it's about the destination. The anxiety begins as I start the car, and I can feel my heart racing as I pull out of the driveway. I carefully plan shopping trips so I do not have to make any left-hand turns to get to a store. I'm an equal

Chapter 13

opportunity right-hand only turner, since I also avoid lefts with gas stations, restaurants, parking lots, and emergency rooms[23].

I know that the moment my foot crosses the threshold of a store, I'll get a headache and my back will feel like I've been in a limbo contest for the last six hours. Between the store doorway and the left-turn thing, you could make a fairly good argument for me being obsessive-compulsive. I'm okay with that; just don't expect me to see a psychologist on the left side of the road.

The solution is online shopping. I still have a lot to learn about finding the best bargains and free shipping, but I'm learning while sitting in an oversized t-shirt and my bunny slippers. I've seen a few people pull off that look at the Uber-Mart, but they are exceptions to the rule.

I just click "forgot your password?" and trust the gods of secure websites not to hand out my credit card information to total strangers, then click on "submit," and voila! I am signed up for daily email notifications of one-day only 40% off markdowns on combination blender/toaster/margarita maker (available in white or camouflage).

One of the biggest dangers is automatic reorder. "We will charge your account quarterly for your next 90-day supply of Wrinkle Ridder." Since this tube costs $90, it

---

[23] If the ER is on the left, keep applying pressure to the wound.

only costs me $1 a day for youthful glowing skin. It would only cost me 67¢ per day to feed a family of five in the Congo, but I go for the cosmetics, in part because I'm too lazy and too forgetful to stop the auto reorder. I'm going straight to hell.

Next time you get your gift basket of mustards from around the world, remember, it's the thought that counts. Just try not to picture me sitting in my underwear while I was thinking of you.

White elephants
Yard sales are your chance to try tripping over somebody else's unwanted stuff at their house before you trip over it at your home. People will attack any yard sale, flea market, or estate sale like piranha on Marlon Brando. The horror, the horror!

My grandparents had no silver or china; no rare coin collections or antique jewelry. What grandpa had were boxes full of pencil stubs and rubber bands. He was the proud owner of a collection of ceramic telephone line insulators and a pantry full of glass-top Bell jars full of thirty-year-old stewed tomatoes.

Grandpa would build a new room onto the house every time he started a new project or hobby. His house had five attics, one of which was only accessible by climbing an apple tree. He died in 1971, and the day of the estate sale one woman in a lime green polyester leisure suit climbed that tree to find the long dormant

Chapter 13

treasures in attic number five. She then proceeded to get into a slap fight with another woman over an antique ice cream parlor chair.

Of all the flea markets and yard sales I've ever been to, there have only been two purchases that brought lasting pleasure. One was a gift coffee mug, which I still use. The other was an eight-inch doll with plastic head, arms and legs; and a white cloth body. My kids bought the doll as a toy for our pet pug, Harold, at our community's yard sale. When Harold wanted to play, he would move his jaw to wiggle a toy enticingly in his mouth.

On the morning of the community yard sale, Harold was tied up in our yard, happily holding the doll by the head. He wiggled his jaw, which caused the dolls legs to frantically kick up and down. The look of horror on shoppers' faces was payback for every boring yard sale I'd ever been forced to endure.

Giant red bow

The first thing I think of when Christmas car commercials begin is not, "What kind of estimated MPG does this car have in the city?" or "How can anyone afford a *car* for a Christmas present?" It is "Where did they find a bow that big?" It's the same every year.

I've been buying cars for a number of years, and practice does not make perfect. Invariably, when I try to haggle over a used car, I end up paying more than the asking price and more than the blue book value. People line up to sell me their cars.

When I'm in the checkout line at a grocery store, I break into a sweat trying to fight the urge to grab handfuls of breath mints and cigarette lighters, so when I took my impulsive self to a car lot, you can imagine what kind of trouble I got into.

Naturally, I bought the first car I test drove. I took the brilliant tack of telling the salesman to give me his best number because I don't haggle … and trusted him to do it. Finally, I cleaned out my savings account so I could pay cash rather than finance.

A   I don't like debt if I can avoid it.
B   I thought I could redeem myself for my poor shopping skills by looking like a high roller to the car dealer. I think I succeeded at looking like an idiot.

"I'll need to go to the credit union. Who should I make the check payable to?" I asked.

"What interest rate are they offering?" The salesman asked. "We have 0% financing for qualified buyers. We can take care of everything right now."

"No, thanks. I'd rather just pay for it today."

(Cricket, cricket)

Now my reputation precedes me at every car dealership in the state. Some consider me a myth or an urban legend, but I really am just that bad at buying a

Chapter 13

car. If I were better at wheeling and dealing, I would have told them to throw in a big red bow.

Green is my favorite color

We live in a world of rampant consumerism. All it takes is one little cockroach in our box of cereal, and we'll throw the whole thing out and get a new box. Now the kids are gone and I'm only shopping for two, it doesn't make sense to buy in bulk. My refrigerator has a row of half-gallon milk cartons lined up in various stages of coagulation. My yogurt and cottage cheese have a thin layer of gray fuzz on top and instead of snapping, my crackers bend. Let's be honest: plastic storage containers are little more than a delayed disposal system.

My grandmother raised a family during the great depression. The woman knew how to stretch a dollar. It turns out grandma was "going green" long before it became fashionable. We grew up in the Seattle area (average rainfall, two gallons a day), but my intrepid grandmother rarely used the dryer on laundry day. Grandma had a clothesline, barn boots, and quick reflexes. She had the boomerang system for leftovers. Those three peas and a kernel of corn would keep coming back to the table each meal until some brave soul "scratched the pot." Grandma darned socks, for Pete's sake. I doubt they still make darning yarn.

I'm going to have to take a page from Grandma's book if I want to actually retire. I suppose I can save some water and turn out all the lights every time I leave a room; I can rinse out and reuse my bread bags; and I can cook up the sack of dried beans that has been in my cupboard for three and a half years.

So far, recycling and reusing has been a matter of good intentions, but at least I've set some realistic goals:

- Use old newspapers to make paper-maché garden gnomes as Christmas gifts for my in-laws
- Bag my produce with double twist ties so I can make jewelry out of the extras
- Share a toothbrush
- Save the product of pooper scooping the yard to start a compost heap on my back porch
- Recycle my used band-aids by using them to wrap Christmas gifts.

I personally might not be the best environmental role model to the next generation, but at least I know how to darn socks.

Chapter 14
Senior Activity Guide

Assuming you have dug enough quarters out from under the couch cushions to retire, you are going to need some new activities to fill your time. If you're not afraid of being blacklisted by PETA, you may want to go hunting or fishing. Up until now, my hunting experience has mainly been small game in the attic. If you're independently wealthy and can lift a bag of cat litter, you can take up golf. If not, there's always water aerobics at the senior center. If exercise is not your thing, what about arts and crafts? I hear the senior center is starting a great new workshop on taxidermy. Bring your own small game from the attic.

The happiest place on earth
There was a time when men would set up a checkerboard on top of a pickle barrel at the general store. They would spend hours playing checkers, swapping gossip, and causing an economic free-fall in the pickle industry. Our modern day equivalent is a bizarre combination of social networking and great prices.

Welcome to Uber-Mart!

If we tried socializing at clubs, the 400-decibel music would render conversation impossible, cause hemorrhaging of the eardrums, and make a Led Zeppelin concert sound like elevator music. At Uber-Mart the music "Cashier to register 12" is easy listening and "Associate needed in sporting goods" always relaxing. Uber-Mart is not a gathering place for hooligans, ne'er-do-wells, or scofflaws. You can wander their aisles at 3:00 in the morning, confident that all the patrons will have shirts and shoes, and that no illegal cold medicine is changing hands in arts and crafts.

On a weekday afternoon, 75% of patrons in any given store are wearing sweat pants. Eva Lutz is wearing shorts that ride up her crotch and bunny slippers. Go ahead and get acquainted, since you'll be seeing a lot of each other over the next few years.

I can't use a fast food restaurant bathroom without buying a bag of fries. Walking out of a store empty-handed would haunt me for months, but I'm getting professional help. If you need purchase-related justification for hanging out at the store, use this simple formula:

- One hour of discussing fishing lures with Rudy Baldwin = 1 pack of Chiclets and 2 AA batteries.
- Three meet & greets in produce = 1 toilet plunger and a scented candle

Chapter 14

- One half hour of watching *The Price is Right* in electronics with anyone who will call out the $1 minimum bid = 1 plastic storage container, a bag of Fritos, and a year's supply of Rice-A-Roni, the San Francisco treat

Finding Uber-Mart buddies is well worth the effort, and is vastly easier than trying to find a pickle barrel.

Gone fishing

I'm only a recent inductee to this time-honored method of wasting time. As a child, I inherited my father's abysmal luck where catching fish was concerned. A typical Sunday of fishing with my dad included:

- 3:30 AM   Wake up
- 3:45 AM   Load the rowboat onto the rusted-out bed of our antique pickup truck
- 4:15 AM   Freeze our asses off on the lake
- 7:00 AM   Still freezing
- 8:30 AM   Load the boat and come home empty-handed
- 10:00 AM   Go to church and thank God we made it through another fishing trip without getting frostbite.

I eventually gave up my bobber in favor of more satisfying pursuits like ironing, until I met my second husband. At the age of 45, in an effort to look interested in his hobbies, I reluctantly tried fishing again ... and discovered *catfish!*

Here was a species of fish practically queuing up[24] to jump onto my line. Deep-sea charter fishing boats fly a marlin flag when entering the marina if somebody on board caught a marlin. I've decided I want a catfish flag for our bass boat, so that as we're puttering up to the dock, I'll be the envy of everyone on shore who only caught blue gills and large mouth bass.

A typical Sunday of senior fishing for my husband and me today includes:

- 11:30 AM   Wake up
- 12:30 PM   Wait for my husband to finish in the bathroom
- 1:00 PM   Still waiting
- 2:00 PM   Go out to breakfast
- 3:30 PM   Hook up the bass boat and head for the river
- 4:00 PM   Launch
- 4:15 PM   Fish
- 5:15 PM   Return to the boat ramp
- 5:30 PM   Hook up the boat and head for home

We practice catch and release because catfish are so ugly it's all I can do to touch them long enough to remove my hook from their gaping mouths. I can't imagine why people would want to go noodling[25] when it means touching the tonsils of the ugly little darlings.

---

[24] A hysterical British colloquialism for "lining up". I get extra credit each time I use the letter "Q" in a sentence.

[25] Getting out of your nice dry boat, diving down to the

Chapter 14

Besides, if you're swimming instead of boating, where are you going to hang the catfish flag?

Call me Bwana

Photo safaris have become a hit among newly retired seniors. Many of our generation were regular devotees of *Mutual of Omaha's Wild Kingdom* every Sunday. What can rival the grace of a gang of angry baboons chasing co-host Jim Fowler while Marlin Perkins offers his whispered narration from off scene?

"Jim will now attempt to avoid the razor sharp teeth of these majestic creatures by swimming across the crocodile-infested Magombo River."

I chose to save money by hunting for big game closer to home. When I went to visit my daughter the other day, she was just waking up. As a string of profanity pierced the morning calm, I rushed into her room. There in the corner was a huge hole in her wall. The new wooden laundry rack she had placed in that corner was chewed to pieces. There was debris from the rack, mixed with leaves, wallboard, and insulation on the floor. The mess had been tracked from the hole into the room, trailing under the bed, where my daughter had been sleeping soundly all night.

To add to the creepiness factor, neither she, nor her two dogs, nor her three cats had woken up during the home invasion. Judging by the size of the hole and the

---

bottom of a muddy river, and using your hand as bait.

height of the chew marks on what was left of the laundry rack, this thing was a beast!

We flew into action, trying to imagine what kind of super rat or stealth opossum could blunder in under the radar. We tried to work out ways to inspect the crawl space under the house without actually going near the entrance. I walked the perimeter of the house looking for footprints leading to the lair under my daughter's bathtub. We blocked off the wall, sealed up the room, and spent the day in the backyard shuddering and thinking up names for the mystery creature. We decided on Bubba.

When the animal removal expert (as seen on the Animal Planet channel) surveyed the damage, he remarked, "#x*&%! We're going to need a bigger cage." After one week without a nibble at the bait, the animal remover sealed up the crawl space and declared the creature gone. I would have liked a picture of Bubba in his natural habitat to add to my photo safari album. I just don't know if Jim Fowler would be able to fit under the house.

In case of a water landing ...
I think it's amusing that airlines refer to crashing into the ocean as "a water landing". If I were actually in the plane during a water landing, the term would apply to the condition of my pants as well as the location of the plane.

Chapter 14

Don't let this ominous possibility deter you from traveling to exotic locations during retirement. Lack of money will be enough of a deterrent.

If you make it to Europe, I would recommend going for a train trip. I rode the train by night and got out to sightsee during the day. If you can work it into your budget, I would *highly* recommend riding in a sleeper car. It beats sharing a cabin with eight French men in a space bristling with luggage and lacking in fresh air.

My only second language is Spanish, but I could tell which country we were in by the announcements on the loudspeaker. In France the train stopped at every "Zshu, Zshu, Zshu" in the country. In Germany, every city was named "Khu, Khu, Khu". I can imagine this made for a lot of confusion on French and German roadmaps. It's a good thing I wasn't driving.

If your budget allows it, go shopping on the streets of the Médina in Marrakesh. If not, go for a picnic in the local park. Life is more of a journey than a destination, so enjoy the scenery, but keep your flotation devices handy and know where the exits are located at all times.

Box of rocks

At one time or another, everybody should bend over and pick up at least one rock. This should be done while four-wheeling in the desert, tramping through the woods, or trespassing on a private island. People who do this regularly as a hobby are referred to as "Rock Hounds," among other epithets.

I have an old Sucrets tin filled with small rocks my grandparents collected during their rock hound phase. It had been some time since I opened my private little treasure chest, so I forgot this was also the depository for the tooth fairy when my kids were little. If I was supposed to throw the teeth away after a specified period, I didn't get the memo. I guess I figured that at some point, I would see these extraneous incisors as precious memories of the time my toddler bit the cat.

I'm pretty sure I will follow in the footsteps of my grandparents and parents in pursuing rock hounding when I retire. It's the ultimate scavenger hunt, requires very little equipment or training, and pays off in big heavy "stuff" you can use to decorate your carport. It gets you out in the sun so you can work on your melanoma and dehydration, and it beats making potholders in a retirement home.

If you get caught trespassing on private property, just claim dementia. You'll be carrying around a box of rocks, so who could doubt your word on the matter?

A hush comes over the gallery
When the Scots started smacking a rock around the field with a stick, I wonder if they knew how popular the "sport" would become? I've had certain benchmarks in

Chapter 14

determining my age through conversations in social settings. Topics included, in chronological order:
- Buying a first house
- Labor and delivery stories
- Bragging about kids
- Strategies for building an investment portfolio
- Golf

I've never played golf on a course that didn't include waterfalls, washboard greens, or windmills. Honestly, I never had a desire to learn golf, and I chuckled to myself when people referred to it as good exercise. More incomprehensible to me than anyone wanting to golf, was anyone wanting to watch other people golf.

Announcer: "Tiger is trying for the triple birdie with a one and a half back flip. This play carries a five-point degree of difficulty ... and a hush comes over the gallery. And he nails it! Execution is flawless and he sticks the landing. Here it is on instant replay."

There are sports that showcase agility, speed, or beating the snot out of your opponent. In 2007, the goalie of hockey's Carolina Hurricanes, Cam Ward, injured his thigh when Brad Isbister "inconsistently" skated over his outstretched leg, slicing the femoral artery. Cam said he didn't feel a thing at the time. The Zamboni driver said many bad words, then asked for a raise.

Announcer: "Due to the graphic nature of the injury, we will turn from the ice to check the crowd's reaction ... and a hush comes over the gallery. Hockey is not a sport for the faint of heart, ladies and gentlemen. For spectators over 50 – please be sure to check with your doctor and take your medication before purchasing a ticket."

If real sports are too much for you, and you've got to watch a (yawn) golf tournament, I recommend you start small. You can watch Sylvia Dinkmeyer sink a par 3 at the windmill. Just don't expect her to do a back flip.

Senior Central
Every retirement community has one: that magical place where all of your free time can be funneled into mindless activity. The senior center at Mom's community is fairly bristling with the accoutrement of gathering, gaming, and exercise.

A pool provides the opportunity for low stress exercises. Swimming laps is a wonderful opportunity for aerobic exercise. I'm a pretty weak swimmer, so my version of aerobic exercise is having an oxygen bottle waiting at either end of the pool. That's about the only way I would be able to get in more than half a lap.

If you've ever dreamed you were Esther Williams, rising out of the pool in the movie *Bathing Beauty*, you can opt for senior synchronized swimming by way of a water aerobics class. Without causing undue stress to arthritic joints, you can bounce around with all the grace of a mermaid in a slow motion water ballet. By mermaid, I'm talking about the nickname for the manatee, a

Chapter 14

lumbering denizen of the not so deep. Their other nickname is "sea cow," but we're not going there.

For me, this is the draw of water aerobics: shallow water. If I don't have to fight to stay afloat, I have enough oxygen to wave my arms and legs around in comically conceived choreography. If you can say that three times fast, you get a cookie. If you actually perform the exercises, you can work off the cookie.

If you want dry land entertainment, every senior center has a shuffleboard court. Here you have a low stress (semi-comatose) opportunity for sliding pucks around the pavement.

Curling is a closely related Canadian game involving stones, ice, brooms, sweepers, and gales of laughter. I'm sure some genius was ahead of his time when he decided sweeping the ice would be a great sport. But walking on ice while shoving stones across the surface is wrong for seniors on so many levels, especially if you're peeing your pants while falling down laughing in zero degree weather.

Most senior centers have a large open hall, which can be used for a popular form of senior entertainment: square dancing. The "dancing" is more like walking around in a bouncy manner. A square is made up of four couples, working together with the precision of a well-planned military operation.

Some cognitive and physical ability is required, and if you are spatially challenged, you might be better off line dancing. Classes are offered for learning the basic movements, combined on the fly and announced by a "caller." So grab your dancing shoes, crank up your hearing aids, and promenade over to the senior center for a bouncy good time.

Go for a stroll

As a kid growing up in the Pacific Northwest, I routinely got the chance to amble down muddy forest trails for miles, looking for some elusive lake or waterfall. My dad insisted we were strolling, since "hiking" was hard. There were many times when strolling became frantically crawling on near vertical slippery slopes. This is the Seattle version of rock climbing.

Walking is considered a stress exercise, and is good for countering the effects of bone loss. It has many aerobic and strength building health benefits. It is not recommended if you are experiencing freezing rain, looting, hot coals, or elk.

My parents would relate to me how the elk would surround their school bus so they weren't able to get off. Mom had nightmares that elk were chasing her through the fields as she was bringing the cows in. I never saw a single wild elk in Washington State until I was in my late 40s. Twenty-five years after moving away from home, I found myself walking on a small road in Packwood, Washington, surrounded by a herd of elk. I figured if I

Chapter 14

kept moving, they would get out of my way, and then I remembered my mom's nightmares.

I froze in the street, trying to channel Marlin Perkins. I didn't have the rudimentary skills to recognize the difference between a bull charging over to gore me, or a cow charging over to trample me. If any elk had flicked an eyelash in my direction, there would be no hope of making it back to the RV with dignity intact. I'm not sure if the screaming sprint is a healthful stress exercise, but all my health concerns at the moment revolved around keeping my spleen intact.

Sexual preference[26]

My preference is short and sweet. I'm not getting any younger, so don't waste my time on getting the right ambience. If I am lying naked on the bed, you can be pretty sure that I am already in the mood.

Even in the best of intimate relationships, sometimes a girl just wants to do the seven basic ballet moves in the shower, while repeatedly taking the name of the Lord in vain.

Detracting from the mood is the fact I break a sweat easily. Between the South Carolina heat, lukewarm water, aerobic exercise, and hot flashes, I'm doomed to smell worse after a date with my shower than I did before. I don't have the energy to take a second shower

---

[26] WARNING: This section contains information of an explicit nature and should not be read by anyone with good taste.

after my heart rate ratchets back down from imminent stroke.

So does age slow down a woman's sex drive? At the very least, it limits the options. Sex in bed sounds better all the time. You can lie down; there is a headboard if you need a handle bar; and you're already on a soft surface in case you need to take a nap afterward (or during).

If my husband is reading this, you rock my world, baby! If my showerhead is reading this, stop texting me. I told you, I'm not in the mood.

Man, some bathroom fixtures just can't take a hint!

Arts and crafts

Every summer growing up I attended Vacation Bible School at my grandma's church. Every year, we took some household object, glued macaroni to it and spray-painted it gold. Whether it was alphabet macaroni on tuna cans or bow tie pasta on ice cream tubs, Mom could count on seeing some form of garish carbohydrate craft.

I wasn't accepted into graphic design school in college because I have very little artistic ability. Placing my "drawings" side by side with those of a real artist, you will see a certain childlike quality in my work. My stuff looks like it rightfully belongs on a refrigerator. My only portrait is a close up of eyelashes.

My grandmother took a painting class and picked up extra tips from a TV art show. She loved to paint the surf or the woods, and she gave me a particularly nice

Chapter 14

woodland scene. What she lacked in talent, she made up for in enthusiasm.

Her painting inspires me now and then to draw an object (usually to stay awake in a meeting) hoping to see that I have suddenly developed an eye for shadows and textures. I'd probably be best starting with basic shapes.

"Why does your picture of a pen look like an egg?" My husband asked.

"That's supposed to be a cell phone."

"Oh. And is that thing the charger?" He tried again.

"That's my empty crockpot." I said. "I know the scale and foreshortening are out of balance, but the message gets across."

"What's the message?"

"If you want dinner, you'll have to call for take out."

Can you dig it?

I have one six-foot fake bamboo plant in my living room and one basket of fake ivy sitting on my shelf. Otherwise, there is nothing remotely botanical looking in my house. The reason is simple: plants hate me. They might not hate me so much if I watered and cared for them, but then we're just getting nit-picky. Other than two perverse African Violets that refused to die, I haven't had much success with houseplants.

Maybe a few of you have been able to go all your lives using dried oregano and parsley flakes without a moment's regret, which just goes to show some people don't have a conscience. I have innumerable books on growing herbs, recognizing herbs and cooking with herbs. What I don't have is ability.

Don't fool yourself. Many herbs like peppermint and sage are basically weeds. One would think I could keep weeds alive, wouldn't one? Even with manure, peat moss, and compost, I couldn't keep chives going for long. For the record, chives are in the onion family and grow in:

- Woodland fields
- Cow pastures
- Indoor pots
- Outdoor pots
- Freeway underpasses
- Drainage ditches
- Cracks in the sidewalk.

So I'm forced to hang my head in shame as I season my potatoes or stir up a pot of spaghetti sauce with freeze-dried herbs.

Combine my gardening disabilities with my washout art skills, and you'll see why the "landscaping" in my yard consists of a tree, a butterfly bush, and one bunch of dead pampas grass. I'm going to re-seed the pampas zone with regular grass seed, but I break out in a rash trying to figure out the best grass seed for the job. For re-seeding my three-foot square patch of dirt, should I stick with the grass variety used by the builders, or research the soil pH and clay content, taking into account

Chapter 14

environmental factors? I'm tempted to stay away from fescue, just because it has a stupid name.

In the end, I'm pretty sure I'm just going to ask the neighbor what he uses and follow along like a horticultural lemming.

Curl up with a good book

I hate to admit it, but I really like a good romance novel. I justify it by making sure the book has some other redeeming quality, like a historical insight. Also, if it's a paranormal romance hybrid it can be considered a guilt-free pleasure. Everybody knows smoldering gazes and heaving breasts are OK if you throw in a vampire or a werewolf.

I'm a slow reader because I'm a very linear thinker. My brain has to sound out each word and translate them all into a story. My lips are moving as I write this.

So *my* test is: if you're surprised to find it's 4:00 in the morning, and your eyes burn so badly they feel like they're bleeding, you know you have a good book. If you keep forgetting to go to the bathroom until you are doing the pee-pee dance, you have a good book. If you forget to eat and your butt falls asleep, you have a *really* good book. When you'd rather read than have sex, it's time to put down the book and invest in a couple bushels of oysters.

The author can give you a carefully detailed description of a place or character, but it is still your mind that makes the story come alive.

Part One:

As Jonathan opened the door, he reached up to his full height and delicately kissed Ginger on the chin. He felt the weight of her gaze and the warmth of her sigh. He looked at the trail from the bath and knew in an instant that she had fallen into her old habits while he was gone.

   a. Jonathan is a little person.
   b. Ginger is his Great Dane.
   c. Ginger had been drinking out of the toilet again.

Part Two:

Unbelievable! How could his girlfriend have forgotten Jonathan would be stopping by that evening? He curled his hands into fists and pounded at her door until the knob rattled. When Eve opened the door, he threw the flowers at her and stomped away.

   a. Jonathan has a poor sense of direction.
   b. Dana is in the lobby.
   c. Eve lives one floor down from Jonathan's girlfriend, Dana.

Part Three:

The night was hot and sticky when Jonathan's buddies came over for poker. A cooler stood next to their

Chapter 14

rooftop table, and the sound of traffic echoed through the alleys. Gary turned to pull some beers out of the cooler as Ed lit his cigar and Jonathan shuffled the deck. There was a scent of sulfur and the air was suddenly alive with a flash of light and a thundering crash.

    a. Jonathan had not checked the weather forecast for that night.

    b. A thunderstorm passed harmlessly to the south.

    c. Gary passed gas as he bent over. When Ed's cigar lit Gary's fart, the explosion could be seen three blocks away.

The great thing about books is that there is always room for interpretation!

LOL

Any signature on a childhood card or letter came with XOXOXOXO. I would send my hugs and kisses to my worst enemy just because it was a cool code. That was the extent of my cryptologic expertise as a child. Who knew shorthand would become the very peanut butter that holds together modern communication? I look at LOL and think, "How sweet. The kids are sending *Lots of Love* the way we used to send hugs and kisses." It doesn't matter how many trivia games tell me it means *Laughing Out Loud*, I'm still going to assume people on Facebook are a little too friendly.

How did we manage all those years to use sarcasm, irony, and puns without some stage direction indicating this was supposed to be funny?

"So Ellen thinks Paul is a total dork. LOL (Laughing out loud)"

"OMG (Oh my God) She wants to have his babies tomorrow. FOTFLOL (Falling on the floor laughing out loud)"

"Can you imagine if Ellen married Paul? Her name would be Ellen Smellen! PMPLOL. (Peeing my pants laughing out loud)"

"I wouldn't want to be one of their kids. FCOL (For crying out loud)"

Is a sense of humor the result of nature or nurture? Some people never seem to laugh, and others think a gaping chest wound is hysterical. I believe everyone has an inborn sense of humor. It can be shaped and influenced by experience, or warped by reading too many *Far Side* comics. At times, humor can even be a choice. There was a time I decided put-down humor was more hurtful than funny. I managed to scrub it from my comedy routine by replacing it with mocking.

Mocking others is completely different and totally fair. This is the reason pretzel vendors at the mall are required to know the Heimlich maneuver. You know those people taking up real estate on mall benches are pointing their mustardy fingers at passersby and

Chapter 14

spewing jalapeño pretzel chunks as they choke with laughter at anyone wearing leg warmers.

"Can you believe she left the house looking like that? Her hair looks like it is trying to run away from her head," Marsha whispered.

"I didn't notice. My eyes were drawn to her coat. That cut and length says 'I'm homeless,'" I replied. "She needs friends who will be brutally honest with her before she is allowed to leave the house."

"You're right. By the way, were you planning on butchering some meat on the way home? All that white you are wearing makes it look like you should be in the packing district."

"Are you kidding? This is my snowstorm ninja look."

It's been proven that laughter is the best medicine. It lowers blood pressure and releases endorphins. It can take our mind off pain and help preserve our sanity when things are going south all around us.

I'm grateful to all the people in my life who keep me laughing, so if you're going to the mall, be sure to wear your leg warmers.

Chapter 15
Stormy Weather

Into every life some rain must fall, back up the sewers, flood the basement, and soak your new $15 a square foot carpet in human waste. Translation: growing old is not for weenies. The sad truth is our age group is considered "expendable" in the workforce, so when your job gets outsourced to Uruguay, you may end up starting your own business. Prepare to hemorrhage money like a gaping chest wound, after you wade through 286 pages of small business tax instructions written in Swahili. If you are working from home, your children will expect you to babysit at a moment's notice. It only takes showing up with earplugs and a bottle of Vodka for your kids to look for other babysitting resources. When your rheumatism can't take the cold and you move to a warmer climate, you'll come face to face with the bane of everyone's existence: spiders the size of fully loaded mini-vans. Seriously, these suckers are big enough to be registered at the DMV (Do More Valium).

Chapter 15

Spamalot

One score and two years ago I started a blog, for the old people, by the old people, conceived in sleep deprivation, and dedicated to the proposition that someone besides my mother may actually read it someday.

In an alarming twist of fate, Nostradamus warned this would be the year of the spammer. SEO engines the world over are churning out messages in ancient Mesopotamian to confound innocent bloggers, who are just trying to make a living by posting ineffectual ads on their websites. I currently have a 3¢ credit with Giggle Add-nonsense.

Quatrain 37.2

> And there shall be a great wind from the east, blowing garbage up the asses of those who would entertain and inform via fiber optic cables and satellite communication. Burma shave.

Spam blocking software on your website runs the risk of sending nasty messages to innocent friends who may occasionally use colorful language in their comments, while allowing messages from users called "Penile Pustules" and "Anal Adventures." What the hell? I still haven't figured out the reasoning behind these programs' determination of what constitutes spam.

You could go the route of demanding your commenters decipher squiggly letters that spell out globfarts, since no machine could ever anticipate such an ambiguous code. I haven't found a globfarts plugin for Wordpress, so I'm left manually deleting messages from XXXewesex and Farmyard_fornication.

For those of you not familiar with SEO (search engine optimization) here's a little primer. Google, Yahoo, Bing, and so forth are popularity contests. If you Google my name, you will find roughly twenty-seven pages of references to me. This is because I am the only Karla Telega in the known universe. As such, the comment I made three months ago concerning toe fungus on your website will be found in Google. Just disregard my link to Beefcake.com. I swear, I thought it was a recipe for meatloaf. Spammers leave comments so they can attach themselves to you like little lampreys, increasing their own visibility. Whew!

I'm so grateful for my readers (shout out to Bob in Dubuque, Iowa) so spam is a small price to pay for my Yahoo ranking of 8,005,563. Woo hoo! During this auspicious year, let us remember that comments from *real* people make all the difference in my own happiness quotient. Comment early, comment often, and I don't even mind if you mention your toe fungus.

Invasion of the ankle biters

I don't want grandchildren. I know, I'll probably get my ass kicked by every woman with a wallet full of photos of Aiden[27] making mud pies. My resolve was reinforced

Chapter 15

recently, when I was put in charge of a two year-old boy for 15 minutes of hell.

We were in a public building, and Mom and Dad were busy filling out paperwork. They put me in charge of their sweet little bundle of attention deficit determination. Within seconds, I lost track of him and turned around just in time to see him pulling letters off the board that read, "Please keep children supervised at all times." The irony was not lost on me.

I used every parenting trick I could remember to keep him from flinging himself down a grassy slope and into the duck pond. What does the bee say? What does the cow say? What is the square root of 139? (Trick question: it's a prime number.) All the while, he trustingly took my hand and dragged me up and down stairs, and into the men's bathroom. The kid has a good grip.

Don't get me wrong. He's a good kid, and no more hyperactive than the average two year-old ... who's just consumed three candy bars and a double espresso. I have no illusion of my ability to catch him if he made a break for it. Fortunately, that's not likely to happen. Lately, small children seem to be attracted to me like flies to poop. They have an innate ability to corner the only adult in a crowded room who doesn't want to pick boogers off their noses.

---

[27] One of the 10 most popular names for boys: really people, get a grip!

I hesitate to even write this. Parents and grandparents get rather miffed if you're not delighted with little "Aiden." I still enjoy visiting my friends who are up to their herniated disks in grandchildren, but even if you rescued me from a burning building, don't expect me to repay the favor by babysitting.

My daughters have been kind enough to let their biological clocks keep ticking. Even though there's no longer any need in this age to clean cloth diapers in boiling bleach, the only bottom I want to wipe is my own. Am I a bad person because I don't want to be around little ankle biters? Just rescue me from a burning building and find out for yourselves.

The Tax Man cometh

The only two constants in life are death and taxes. One might argue death is the worse of the two, but it only comes around once in your life. Taxes accrue every year, culminating in the April 15 midnight scramble at the post office. There have been many times, while hunched over my Form 1040, that I have prayed for the sweet release of death. The same could be said for waiting in line at the Post Office on December 23, but that's another story.

Dear Mr. IRS Agent: Please find below my 2012 tax return.

Chapter 15

KARLA TELEGA			2L8-4U-2RUN
Additions to income			
7	Wages, salaries, tips, etc.	Writer	0.
8a	Taxable Interest		NKA
12b	Off-track betting		0.
12c	Money laundering	Not yet	0.
15	Total Income		0.
Subtractions from income			
17	Childcare expenses	No, thanks	0.
21	Railroad benefits		0.
22	Clown school		10.
36dd	Business expenses	Toner Cartridge	2,368.
43	Total Expenses		2,378.
43 ½	Total Taxable Income		(2,378).
44	Tax	New math	Right kidney
61	Federal Tax withheld		0.
64	Total payments owed	Visa	Credit limit

If you were able to keep up, congratulations! You've just won the job of doing taxes for all your friends.

I worked briefly as a mortgage loan processor, where I reviewed borrowers' federal tax returns. Once I conquered schedule C, I figured I had learned everything there was to know about the tax code ... and I got cocky. (Have you noticed a pattern emerging here?)

Thank goodness my husband does our taxes online, because it turns out I'm not so good at it.[28] This year I've become self-employed (code for "out of work"). Now my filing status is changing, I decided to read the book.

The instructions for Form 1040 are a mere 174 pages of unintelligible and mind numbing legalese. I love how each new year's publication starts out with "What's new for 2012" (or whatever new tax year you have the misfortune of reading about). The fatal flaw with this statement is it assumes I know what's old for 2012.

I spent an hour and a half on the phone with a very helpful IRS representative to learn more about my new filing status. He gave me the numbers of five different instructional publications specifically for starting up a new business.

He told me, "It sounds like a lot of reading, but it's really no more than about half a Bible."

I'm not sure to this day if that was IRS humor, or if he was serious.

I would like to see an illustrated tax manual. If I could see a picture of a smiling taxpayer hitting "send" to allow the IRS electronic access to his life savings, I might be more tempted to save paper and file electronically. There could be a picture of smiling IRS agents with

---

[28] Let me assure any IRS agents reading this book that I have never cheated on my taxes. Egregious errors I can't swear to.

Chapter 15

rubber hoses, locked in a small room conducting an audit with a happy taxpayer. I would read a publication like that, as long as it was no longer than half a Bible.

Stayin' alive

Recently I had to go to the DMV twice in one week, because one day of torture is never enough. Like roughly 97% of the customers at the DMV on that Wednesday, I was turned away as a suspected terrorist, as evidenced by my lack of proof of insurance.

It seems my insurance company neglected to send the official electronic okey-dokey, to prove I was paying out the nose for my chance to spend a huge deductible if my car door gets dinged in the parking lot. With just one phone call, three customer service reps with thick accents, and twenty minutes of elevator music, I found someone willing to flip the magical switch at the insurance company.

There are specific things you can do to make another wasted day at the DMV more interesting. Before walking in, you need to paste a creepy smile on your face. It makes the workers there wonder what you're thinking. If you reach into your coat pocket for a used Kleenex, you'll get to watch them all duck and cover.

The workers themselves are carefully trained never to crack a smile. Their permitted facial expressions range from angry, to comatose. Anyone caught being cheerful has to administer driving tests to the blind. You have only to try to merge onto the expressway to know there are many visually impaired drivers on South Carolina roads. Obviously, they all had proof of insurance.

Short of self-medication prior to "take a number," there is little you can do to make your trip to the DMV more pleasurable. I plan on starting a sing-along for all the people numbers D148 to D316. If we all hold hands and sing Kumbaya interminably, maybe the workers will be motivated to keep the line moving along and get us out of there.

If you don't hear from me by Monday, you'll know I'm either still at the DMV, or I've been incarcerated for singing folk songs from the 60s in public. I hope they don't throw me in the same cell with the people who are missing their marriage licenses. They tend to be Bee Gees fans. I can only take so much "Saturday Night Fever."

Daddy long legs
One of the advantages of living in the south is that it's not the north. Winter no longer carries the risk of death from hypothermia while walking from your house to your car. One of the disadvantages of living in the south is spiders. I hate spiders! I wasn't born with a natural fear and loathing, but experience has taught me you don't want to get within hopping distance of one. Don't try to tell me that spiders don't hop. With a magnifying glass you would be able to see the anticipation in all the little

Chapter 15

lenses of their compound eyes, and the gnashing of their venom-filled fangs each time a person gets within range.

I recently took on the challenge of cleaning the screened porch. This involved sweeping away cobwebs along the roofline while standing directly underneath them. Tiny strands and egg sacks were flying every direction and I was at ground zero. I struggled to be strong and not beg for rescue each time I had to gish a live one. I couldn't wait to strip out of my shorts and t-shirt so I could take a shower with boiling bleach.

When I went to bed the night after my ordeal, I felt some discomfort in my yoo-hoo area. I was itching and scratching in a most un-ladylike manner. Fortunately, as we all know, scratching is acceptable as long as you are under the covers with the lights out. Finally, I turned on the light to investigate and found a spider bite right where my panties meet my inner thigh. Let me be perfectly clear: there had been a spider IN MY PANTS! Thank God for those extra middle-age pounds that kept my panty elastic stretched tighter than shrink wrap, forming an impenetrable barrier between my lady parts and any eight-legged creatures.

I should be used to icky bugs by now. I live in the Low Country of South Carolina where they grow free-range spiders as big as saucers. Dogs and cats under fifteen pounds have mysteriously disappeared without a trace in areas frequented by these Goliaths. No spider has been caught in the act yet, but if you go to the bar, you can hear them bragging to each other about their latest conquest.

A walk through the woods involves a lookout man with a baseball bat, and a revolver. On one such walk, my son stopped to do what guys normally do when confronted by alligators, snakes, and giant spiders: he poked one of these monsters with a stick. I swear I am telling the truth. The spider grabbed the stick and took it away from him. Then he shook the stick menacingly at my son. Even the armed and dangerous lookout man wasted no time getting back to the car.

I don't want to discourage anyone from visiting our beautiful state, but you might want to stay out of the woods and off of my back porch when you come.

Revenge of epidemic proportions
This is a public service announcement from the Center for Disease Control.

To the cranky looking representative at the DMV:

You know, yesterday, when I felt like crap: I didn't drag my bronchitis-riddled self to your establishment just so you could lose my paperwork somewhere between counter seven and the camera. I'm hoping the woman with the walker sitting next to me had her flu shot, because I hacked up enough sputum in your establishment to have the CDC descend on the place with haz-mat suits.

Chapter 15

To the teller who insisted on putting a three-day hold on my check:

You probably don't want to know how many snotty Kleenex tissues I was handling with the same paws that handed you the check and my driver's license. It was a lot.

Unfortunately, the world does not stand still when you're sick. The good thing about working from home is that I no longer have co-workers walking by my desk and macing me with Lysol as they pass. At home, I can chug down enough codeine so that I don't remember whether it's standard time or daylight savings time (help me out here, folks) and nobody will be the wiser.

I have about a two-day limit of patience for listening to people whine when they're sick, myself included, so I try to space it out. Yesterday, I indulged in a full day funk. I was pouty, impatient, and petulant: the trifecta of annoying. If they had put the damn whipped cream and a cherry on top of my chocolate milkshake, I probably would have spontaneously combusted right there in the soda shop.

So my apologies to Ms. Cranky-Pants at the DMV. I wasn't in the best of moods myself while snorting phlegm at your counter. Today I don't have to drive, so I can stay at home, chug my codeine, and avoid exposing others to contagion and misery. Although, Ms. Bank

Teller, you put a hold on my check: you kinda had it comin'.

I'll see you next August

Time once again for my annual lament at the passing of a great American pastime. I'm sad to see the football season winding down to an end for another year. This is going to put a major crimp in my sex life.

Every Sunday, my husband and I celebrate naked football day. We like to have the game going while we scrump like bunnies, because at our age, it helps to hear the crowd cheering us on. It's nice to know the defensive players are also exhausted by the third drive and sucking wind. Of course, we never make it to a third drive.

Two years ago after the Super Bowl, we were desperate to have some kind of background noise from the TV, so we randomly chose a channel. Up came Norm Abrams on *The New Yankee Workshop*. Norm got his television start as a carpenter on *This Old House*, an old favorite of mine.

On this occasion, Norm was building a chest, and explaining how to put together the drawers. I heard snatches as we struggled for inspiration. "Notice the dovetailing ..." I blushed.

He was relentless. "Now we're going to take the router ... tongue in groove ..." Okay, that's it. I was officially weirded-out. We lost our place, and were too

Chapter 15

embarrassed to even snuggle. I did the walk of shame into the bathroom to get dressed.

In February, we start naked NASCAR. I get a little thrill when I hear, "Gentlemen, start your engines." On top of the cheering, we get to hear the thunder of unlimited horsepower. My only stipulations are: no drafting, and no bump and run.

A Purple Dress that Doesn't Suit me Well
When I told my friends I was going to join the Red Hat Society, they took the news pretty well. My family, hoping it was just a passing fancy, didn't hold an intervention. My best friend only offered nominal resistance when I signed her up, while my son took delight in making up totally unjustified urban myths about the society.

Coming back from the beach, my son and I passed a prison work crew picking up litter. The group included a woman who appeared to be in her early 60s. Mark told me she was Agnes, the Sergeant-at-Arms for the local Red Hat chapter. People gave her a wide berth on the prison grounds after she shivved a guard for confiscating her cigarettes. Pointing out the fact red and purple were gang colors, he told me that for the initiation I'd have to go to Jacksonville and act as wheel man in a hit.

What a crock! Even when we rumble at the local watering hole, at worst we're only coffee-swilling hooligans and scofflaws, passing around mug shots of grandchildren, and cookie recipes. That rumor about the goat rampage at the library is totally unfounded. The riot never made it outside of the petting zoo.

In 2012, 35% of Americans were aged fifty and older. The AARP estimates an even higher percentage. Little wonder the hormonally challenged are banding together just to hang out and laugh at themselves. We don't want to promote nudism, put a woman on the moon, or complain about the weather. We just want to have fun and make poor fashion choices. And if we occasionally take a trip to Jacksonville, you never heard it from me.

Strutting your stuff downtown

Is there a correlation between blushing and spontaneous combustion? I'm afraid if I read *Fifty Shades of Gray*, I might find out. I'm kind of a vanilla girl, so I admit to some ignorance about safe words, harnesses, and why some people spend good money to see Carrot Top.

I pride myself on an extensive vocabulary, so I was surprised yesterday, when my daughter used a word I've never heard before: merkin. I blame it on my revulsion at watching The Real Housewives of Anywhere. Apparently, one of these women sells merkins.

I looked up merkin on Wikipedia, and was nearly blinded by a picture of a hot pink hairpiece pasted to a woman's lady parts. A merkin is a pube wig!! Even though I'm genetically predisposed to post-menopausal

Chapter 15

hair loss, there is no way I'm going to walk around with dryer lint glued to my naughty parts.

The first step in wearing a merkin is to have all your God-given hair south of the navel yanked out by the roots. Merkins are for people who like to shake it up with different colors and textures. PETA has recently issued statements condemning the use of animal fur to cover these particular bald spots, although they were blushing as they said it.

Yes, you can purchase a fox or mink merkin. Personally, if I had mink, I'd have my hand down my pants 24/7. I can just imagine the indignant look on the fox who learned his fur would be used as a human hall runner.

Love's labor misplaced
My only credentials for writing are a Bachelor's degree in Spanish Literature, a job in high school as yearbook editor, and a library card. I never planned on authoring a book because it sounded hard. It turns out I love to write, although by now you've figured out I art not Shakespeare.

Since I told family and friends of my intention to write this book, I've learned many of them also want to write. They're just not crazy and impulsive enough to quit their day jobs to take up the pen.

Do something you love and you'll never work. Retirement doesn't have to be reserved exclusively for Bingo and bake sales unless:

- Baking is what you truly love
- You live in my neighborhood
- You make killer cinnamon rolls. (Call me.)

I recommend you keep an open mind about what constitutes "play". This may be your chance to do what you've had in the back of your mind for years. If what you've had in the back of your mind is farmyard fornicating, I don't want to hear about it. You can go straight to confession without even kicking any puppies on the way.

Chapter 16
Getting More Bang for your Bucket List

Those of us in the baby boomer demographic are considered seniors with training wheels, but if you haven't had your fifteen minutes of fame yet, you'd better get on it. One possibility: Vinnie's House of Hedonism is giving a free Margarita to anyone who can sing all the lyrics to *Bye-Bye Miss American Pie*. This is also the perfect time to simplify your life, best achieved by bestowing all your old useless crap on someone less fortunate. This serves the dual purpose of giving you brownie points, and having room to park your mid-life crisis in the garage. After that, there's nothing left but to refuse to grow up. I'm getting a late start on writing, but I still have at least a good twenty years worth of third grade potty humor left in me. I wouldn't want it go to waste.

Making a splash
I've tried to think of where a fairly anonymous figure can be in the limelight for fifteen minutes of fame. The obvious conclusion is a karaoke bar. Here is a group of people in various stages of inebriation, willing to listen to

me wail out *The Wreck of the Edmund Fitzgerald.* Even when I'm old and my voice sounds like an LP (yes, that's a vinyl record) that's been dragged through a rock quarry, who will know the difference?

Sometimes the easiest solution is the most elegant. I'm speaking, of course, about getting into the Guinness Book of World Records. Popular categories include:

- World's largest pencil stub collection (my grandpa holds the current title)
- World's worst meat loaf (talk to my mom)
- World's tightest shorts (go to the Uber Mart any Sunday)
- World's largest Johnson (call me)

If I play to my strengths, I'd go for the largest number of unfinished projects. I know there are many people who start things they don't finish, but I think my pile of half-ass mending puts me right up there.

Every time I go all Martha Stewart and invest in felt, a hot glue gun, gold spray paint, and eight packs of pipe cleaners,[29] my husband groans. He knows he's not going to see the kitchen table for at least three months.

As long as Muriel Gunderson doesn't enter with her 464 half-finished Kleenex flowers, I might have a shot. If not, I always know where to go if I get a runny nose.

---

[29] Used to make Christmas ornaments, or a dirty bomb.

Chapter 16

Pay it forward

Remember in third grade, when Danielle let you win at tetherball on the playground? Neither do I. Actually, Danielle was the one who gave the whole class head lice. Nevertheless, odds are that by now, most of us have been on the receiving end of kindness from others. Even if you haven't fallen down an open manhole (who hasn't?) there are dozens of opportunities for people to help you. They can:

- rescue you from a burning outhouse
- give you their seat in the back of the police car
- babysit your pet wolverine
- donate to CFW "Cheese for Writers" (Contributions are tax deductible).

In the cosmic scheme of things, we are now under some sort of contractual obligation to repay the favor[30]. We do this by forcing our benevolence on innocent bystanders. I refer to this as STANK (Stealth Tactical Ambush of Nominal Kindness).[31]

Others may be opportunistic, looking for that moment when someone is in need, and pouncing on them like a premenstrual woman on a Milky Way bar. It isn't pretty. I prefer to be prepared to carry out my mission with military precision. When my husband yelled at me that our elderly neighbor had fallen in the

---

[30] And your pet-sitter's emergency room bill

[31] Fifteen years in the military service, and that's the best acronym I could come up with.

driveway, I was out of the house in a flash with the ambulance on speed dial. I came equipped with a towel, a standard first aid kit, a flashlight, and a mimosa. Hey, I was thirsty.

The keyword here is "nominal." If you overdo it, you might tear a muscle. Be sure to lift with your legs when you're picking up the newspaper your neighbor dropped because her arms were loaded down with five bags of groceries and a toddler.

The hardest part of STANK is that you're not supposed to expect anything in return. If the man on the bus doesn't thank you for your unsolicited advice on the best place to get a toupee that doesn't look like fresh road kill, you have to take it with grace and simply be satisfied with a job well done.

This is your chance to get those good Samaritan warm and fuzzies. As we get older, we want to know we left our mark on the world. The best (and cheapest) way is to leave behind a legacy of STANK victims. You will be a better person for it. Plus, I hear it gives you immunity to head lice.

Simply delightful

Every time I moved, I would open a box of my crappy old stuff and feel like it was Christmas morning. "Oh look, the can of olives I bought in 1992!" (Shut up! It has sentimental value.) I'd really like to simplify my life, but

Chapter 16

you'll have to pry that olive can out of my cold, dead fingers.

Once you kick the kids out of the nest, change the locks, and hire a bouncer to watch the front door, it's time to consider downsizing. Do you really need to clean four toilets, six closets, and a double car garage? Why are you saving the size six jeans that stopped fitting about the time you started hot flashes?

I'm not suggesting you move to the country and can your own pickles (dill spears). I just think there are so many things we can do without and still be happy. If you save your used candy bar wrappers, there's no hope for you. Just sayin'.

The problem with this theory is that I really like my stuff. How can I part with all the duplicate toenail clippers? I've got a leg up on some people, since my fine china has the word "Dixie" stamped on it.

I try to will myself into throwing stuff away. I may as well resolve not to snore or sleep with my mouth hanging open. Wanting it doesn't stop me from being a candidate for a ridiculous You-tube video when I'm napping on the couch. What I need is a concrete plan.

For starters, I could do without:

Spammers, twenty pounds, rude customer service representatives, trips to the mall, elevator music, and horseradish. I'm already well on my way towards a simpler lifestyle. I'm open to suggestions on what else to eliminate. I don't have all the answers, but at least I have my olives.

The Peter Pan Principle

You've spent enough of your lives being responsible adults. I believe every senior should have a Mr. Potato Head right up until the day he dies. (A Cootie game is also acceptable.) If you haven't reached retirement age yet, you don't have to wait to become semi-irresponsible kids. I like to take retirement test runs. If you find an isolated stream to go skinny-dipping, be sure to use the buddy system. If you find a public fountain, I'll pretend I don't know you, and don't hold your breath waiting for me to post bail.

Never growing up means I don't need all the answers. This is fortunate, since I frequently don't remember the questions. I like when I can recapture that childlike curiosity about the world around me. I don't like early bedtimes, soft foods, or accidents.

Time might be putting some limitations on our bodies, but it doesn't have to limit our outlook.

"Hey, Babe. Is there anything good on TV?" my husband muttered.

"Just reruns. Why don't we go to the beach?"

He sat up straighter. "Because it's 10:00 PM and forty-two degrees out."

"You can't run a clandestine operation during the middle of the day. This way, they'll never see us

Chapter 16

coming." I hurried to the closet for my coat. "You get the clam shovels and I'll bring the flashlights!"

"We don't even know if it's low tide."

I shrugged. "That's the idea. We'll keep them guessing."

Later, as we walked along the beach, my husband took my hand and said, "Do you know what would make this night even better?"

"What?"

"Third grade potty humor," he replied.

We looked at each other and simultaneously said, "Speufar."

Acknowledgments

My special thanks to Art and Robin Nichols of Nichols Equipment, who let me crawl around on one of their bulldozers. I couldn't figure out how to drive it, much to the relief of the Moncks Corner police department and local citizens. Thanks also to my editor, Rosanne Dingli, who keeps me from making a total fool of myself. Not an easy task. Finally, thanks to my loving family. You help me walk that narrow road between egomania and self doubt. Well done!

Thanks to El Kartun for his extraordinary cover art. www.elkartun.zirculomarketing.com

About the Author

Award winning author of *Box of Rocks*, blogger extraordinaire, humor writer, and professional napper. As a graduate of hot flashes, Karla Telega considers herself a champion of the youth-impaired. She is a six-year survivor of Southern living. (Seriously, you should see the size of some of these spiders.) She lives with her husband in South Carolina where she enjoys reading, watching cheesy Sci-Fi movies, and taking long-ish walks. You can read more adventures in aging at her humor blog, Telega Tales. telegatales.com

www.ingramcontent.com/pod-product-compliance
Lightning Source LLC
Chambersburg PA
CBHW061427040426
42450CB00007B/939